Wishing you a
happy birthday
Robert, Tina, Robert William +
Catherine
x x T

D1491786

What a
Wonderful World

❋ ❋ ❋

Also by Fiona Castle

CANCER'S A WORD, NOT A SENTENCE
RAINBOWS THROUGH THE RAIN

*

Compiled by Fiona Castle and Rob Parsons

MY FAMILY

What a Wonderful World

***

AN ANTHOLOGY OF JOY

Fiona Castle

Hodder & Stoughton
LONDON   SYDNEY   AUCKLAND

British Library Cataloguing in Publication Data
A record for this book is available from
the British Library

ISBN 0 340 75615 2

Printed and bound in Great Britain
by Clays Ltd, St Ives plc

Hodder and Stoughton
A division of Hodder Headline Ltd
338 Euston Road
London NW1 3BH

Contents

❋ ❋ ❋

Acknowledgments

---

* * *

While every effort has been made to contact the copyright holders of material used in this book, this has not always been successful. Full acknowledgment will gladly be made in future editions.

We gratefully acknowledge the following:

ABBA, 'Thank you for the music', used with permission by Bocu Music Ltd.

Eddie Askew, 'Facing the Storm', used with permission of The Leprosy Society.

John Betjeman, 'A Subaltern's Love-Song', used with permission by John Murray Publishers Ltd.

Phil Collins, 'Another Day in Paradise', used with permission by Hit and Run Music Publishing Ltd.

Bill Cosby, *Time Flies.* © Bill Cosby and published by Bantam Press, a division of Transworld Publishers. All rights reserved.

Sylvia Dee, 'Bring me sunshine', used with permission by International Music Network.

Kathy Frizzell and Claire Cloninger, 'My Song in the Night', copyright © 1990 Word Music. Administered by CopyCare, P.O. Box 77, Hailsham, BN27 3EF music@copycare.com. Used by permission.

Acknowledgments

Graham Kendrick & Steve Thompson, 'Teach me to dance', copyright © (1993) Make Way Music, PO Box 263, Croydon, Surrey, CR9 5AP, UK. International copyright secured. All rights reserved. Used by permission.

Graham Kendrick, 'Who can sound the depths of sorrow', copyright © (1988) Make Way Music, PO Box 263, Croydon, Surrey, CR9 5AP, UK. International copyright secured. All rights reserved. Used by permission.

Frances Moore Lappé, Joseph Collins and Peter Rosset, *World Hunger: 12 Myths*, © (1998) Earthscan. Used by permission.

Susan Lenzkes, *No Rain, No Gain*, © 1995. Used by permission of Discovery House Publishers, Box 3566, Grand Rapids MI 49501, USA. All rights reserved.

Aub Podlich from *Beyond the Trees*. Used by permission of Openbook Publishers.

Tricia Richards, 'The Artist', used with permission of the author.

Harry Secombe, *Strawberries and Cream*, published by Jerome Robson and used with permission.

Vera Sinclair, 'In praise of Trees', used with permission of *This England* magazine.

Paul Francis Webster (words) and Sammy Fain (music), 'Love is a many-splendoured thing'. © 1955 Catalogue Partnership/EMI Miller Catalogue Inc., EMI USA. Worldwide print rights controlled by Warner Bros Publications Inc/IMP Ltd. Reproduced by permission of International Music Publications Ltd.

George Weiss and Bob Theile, 'What a Wonderful World', used with permission from Carlim Music Corp and Memory Lane Music.

What a Wonderful World

***

I see trees of green, red roses too
I see them bloom for me, for you
And I think to myself
What a wonderful world.

I see skies of blue and clouds of white
The bright blessed day – the dark sacred night
And I think to myself
What a wonderful world.

 The colours of the rainbow so pretty in the sky
Are also on the faces of people going by.
I see friends shaking hands, saying 'How do you do?'
They're really saying, 'I love you.'

 I hear babies cry, I watch them grow
They'll learn much more than I'll ever know
And I think to myself
What a wonderful world,
Yes, I think to myself
What a wonderful world.

Louis Armstrong

CHAPTER ONE

A celebration of life

❋ ❋ ❋

The moment I was asked to write an anthology on 'A Celebration of Life' I knew that 'Wonderful World' would have to be the centrepiece! Louis Armstrong sings it with such warmth and compassion, and captures the wonder of God's creation. It was one of my husband Roy's favourites too and many a time he sang it for an audience in cabaret. It was an obvious choice if someone was celebrating the birth of a new baby or an engagement.

I recently discovered a recording by Louis Armstrong on a CD which also included the following message by him. I will write it as it sounds, so picture as you read it the well-worn face and the rich, mellow gravelly tones of his then ageing voice and you will capture the heart of what he is saying ...

Some of you young folks bin saying to me, 'Hey, Pops, what do you mean – "what a wonderful world"? How about all them wars all over the place – ya call them wonderful? And how about hunger and pollution – them ain't so wonderful either.' Then how about listening to old Pops for a minute.

Seems to me it ain't the world that's so bad
but what we're doing to it and all I'm saying
is see what a wonderful world it would be if
only we'd giv'n it a chance – luuuve … baby
luuuve – that's the secret – yeahhh.

If lots more of us loved each other we'd
solve lots more problems and, man … This
world would be a gassa! That's what ol' Pops
keeps saying.

*L*ouis Armstrong puts his finger right on the
button when he says that love is the secret. After
all the Bible tells us that we should love God with
all our hearts and love our neighbours as ourselves.

One of the most famous Bible passages, read at
many weddings, is from Paul's first letter to the
Corinthians, chapter 13.

If I could speak in any language in heaven or
on earth but didn't love others, I would only
be making meaningless noise like a loud
gong or a clanging cymbal. If I had the gift
of prophecy, and if I knew all the mysteries
of the future and knew everything, but
didn't love others, what good would I be?
And if I had the gift of faith so that I could
speak to a mountain and make it move,
without love I would be no good to
anybody. If I gave everything I have to the
poor and even sacrificed my body, I could
boast about it but if I didn't love others, I
would be of no value whatsoever.

Love is patient and kind. Love is not jealous or boastful or proud or rude. Love does not demand its own way. Love is not irritable, and it keeps no record of when it has been wronged. It is never glad about injustice but rejoices whenever the truth wins out. Love never gives up, never loses faith, is always hopeful, and endures through every circumstance.

Love will last forever, but prophecy and speaking in unknown languages and special knowledge will all disappear. Now we know only a little, and even the gift of prophecy reveals little! But when the end comes, these special gifts will all disappear.

It's like this: When I was a child, I spoke and thought and reasoned as a child does. But when I grew up, I put away childish things. Now we see things imperfectly as in a poor mirror, but then we will see everything with perfect clarity. All that I know now is partial and incomplete, but then I will know everything completely, just as God knows me now.

There are three things that will endure – faith, hope, and love – and the greatest of these is love.

I remember being asked to substitute my own name in place of the word 'love' in the second paragraph. A humbling experience! But then substitute it with Jesus' name and it gives us a measure of His enduring love for us.

Love isn't love till you give it away.

Oscar Hammerstein

Just before my husband died, my son Benjamin was playing the tune of this hymn at the piano. Roy asked him to repeat it again and again, saying it was one of his favourite hymns. The words bear out the message of Jesus' love for us.

My song is love unknown,
My Saviour's love to me,
Love to the loveless shown, that they might lovely
   be.
O who am I, that for my sake
My Lord should take frail flesh and die?

He came from his blest throne,
Salvation to bestow:
But men made strange and none the longed-for
   Christ would know.
But O, my Friend, my Friend indeed;
Who at my need his life did spend!

Sometimes they strew his way,
And his sweet praises sing:
Resounding all the day hosannas to their King.
Then 'Crucify!' is all their breath,
And for his death they thirst and cry.

In life, no house, no home
My Lord on earth might have;
In death, no friendly tomb but what a stranger gave.
What may I say? Heav'n was his home:
But mine the tomb wherein he lay.

Here might I stay and sing,
No story so divine;
Never was love, dear King, never was grief like thine!
This is my Friend, in whose sweet praise
I all my days could gladly spend.

Samuel Crossman

Keep love in your heart.
A life without it
is like a sunless garden …
The consciousness of loving
and being loved
brings a warmth
and richness to life
that nothing else can bring.

Oscar Wilde

CHAPTER TWO

I see trees of green ...

❋ ❋ ❋

O DREAMY GLOOMY FRIENDLY TREES

O dreamy gloomy friendly trees,
I came along your narrow track
to bring my gifts unto your knees
And gifts you did give back;
For when I brought this heart that burns –
These thoughts that bitterly repine –
And laid them here among the ferns
And the hum of boughs divine
Ye vastest breathers of the air,
Shook down with slow and mighty poise
Your coolness on the human care
Your wonder on its toys,
Your greenness on the heart's despair
Your darkness on its noise.

Herbert Trench

IN PRAISE OF TREES

Without the Oak, no beam in ship or hall
Without the Pine, no stately mast at all
Without the Elm, no barns to store the hay
Without the Chestnut no counter games to play
Without the Walnut, no furniture to make.

Without the Ash, no oars to row the boat
Without the trees, no place to build a home
for nesting birds when early spring is come
Without the trees no blossom time to bring
from year to year the promise of spring
Without the trees, no shade of summer heart
Without the trees no juicy fruits to eat
We all need trees, protect them please!

Vera Sinclair

Nature gives to every time and season some
beauties of its own; and from morning to
night, as from the cradle to the grave, is but
a succession of change so gentle and easy
that we can scarcely mark their progress.

Charles Dickens

Praise the LORD, I tell myself; O LORD my God, how
    great you are!
You are robed with honour and with majesty; you are
    dressed in a robe of light.
You stretch out the starry curtain of the heavens; you
    lay out the rafters of your home in the rain clouds.
You make the clouds your chariots; you ride upon
    the wings of the wind.
The winds are your messengers; flames of fire are
    your servants.

You placed the world on its foundation so it would
    never be moved.
You clothed the earth with floods of water, water
    that covered even the mountains.
At the sound of your rebuke, the water fled; at the
    sound of your thunder, it fled away.
Mountains rose and valleys sank to the levels you
    decreed.
Then you set a firm boundary for the seas, so they
    would never again cover the earth.

You make the springs pour water into ravines, so
    streams gush down from the mountains.
They provide water for all the animals, and the wild
    donkeys quench their thirst.
The birds nest beside the streams and sing among the
    branches of the trees.
You send rain on the mountains from your heavenly
    home, and you fill the earth with the fruit of your
    labour.
You cause grass to grow for the cattle.You cause
    plants to grow for people to use.You allow them
    to produce food from the earth –
wine to make them glad, olive oil as a lotion for their
    skin, and bread to give them strength.
The trees of the LORD are well cared for – the cedars
    of Lebanon that he planted.
There the birds make their nests, and the storks make
    their homes in the firs.
High in the mountains are pastures for the wild
    goats, and the rocks form a refuge for rock
    badger.

You made the moon to mark the seasons and the sun
    that knows when to set.
You send the darkness, and it becomes night, when
    all the forest animals prowl about.
Then the young lions roar for their food, but they
    are dependent on God.
At dawn they slink back into their dens to rest.
Then people go off to their work; they labor until the
    evening shadows fall again.

O LORD, what a variety of things you have made! In
    wisdom you have made them all. The earth is full
    of your creatures.
Here is the ocean, vast and wide, teeming with life of
    every kind, both great and small.
See the ships sailing along, and Leviathan, which you
    made to play in the sea.
Every one of these depends on you to give them
    their food as they need it.
When you supply it, they gather it.You open your
    hand to feed them, and they are satisfied.
But if you turn away from them, they panic.
When you take away their breath, they die and turn
    again to dust.
When you send your Spirit, new life is born to
    replenish all the living of the earth.

May the glory of the LORD last forever! The LORD
    rejoices in all he has made!
The earth trembles at his glance; the mountains burst
    into flame at his touch.

Psalm 104

O Earth! thou hast not any wind that blows
Which is not music; every weed of thine
Pressed nightly flows in aromatic wine;
And every humble hedgerow flower that grows,
And every little brown bird that doth sing,
Hath something greater than itself, and bears
A living word to every living thing,
Albeit it holds the message unawares.
All shapes and sounds have something which is not
Of them: a Spirit broods among the grass;
Vague outlines of the Everlasting Thought
Lie in the melting shadows as they pass;
The touch of an Eternal Presence thrills
The fringes of the sunsets and the hills.

Richard Realf

O LORD, open my lips, and my mouth will
declare your praise.

Psalm 51:15

I have never been very impressed with the old argument that the beauty of a flower, or the order of a beehive, ought to convince people that there is a God. It seems perfectly logical to me that my humanist friends, on inspecting the intricate construction of a banksia, or enjoying the serenity of a forest, should simply enthuse: 'Isn't nature marvelous!' or 'Hasn't evolution excelled itself!' Having approached the world from a scientific, rational point of view, how could they come to any other conclusion? The truth is that nobody has yet been converted by a waratah or a mountain ash.

Science, reason, a sense of beauty and order, and just common old eyesight – all these great gifts – all add to our appreciation of nature as *God's* world only after we have first come to God through other means. When I know God, then every leaf drips with him. When I know him, I know him everywhere. All knowledge and beauty and order become 'baptised', and the heavens themselves declare his glory, not to mention the cane toads and earthworms!

God is first found not by eyes, but by ears. Nobody 'thinks' their way to God; nobody 'discovers' him. The more you look or think the more distant and improbable he becomes. Yes, you will see God in every tree and raindrop – but first you must meet him in that different dimension where he is met: in that other world, the world of the Spirit.

That world cannot be entered by breaking through from the outside. It must be opened by the One inside it. God opens windows to his world, through which we may see him, and from which his light shines, to be seen on grass, flowers, and grains of sand. God's windows always reduce to just one thing, to that one Person who is known as his Word. 'Faith comes from hearing ... the word of Christ' (Romans 10:17).

Against the ear of that person who has already been moved to want to know God, God lays his mouth. God speaks. In the speaking, God comes. The speaking God has already come down to be very close. He lays his mouth against your ear! When he does that, he is about to perform in you the miracle he has already performed many times in the whole creation: to make something out of nothing.

When God speaks, as One close to you, it is his very closeness which opens your eyes to the great distance, as vast as the universe, that stretches between you and him. This is what the ancient poet of Genesis kept emphasizing when he assigned God all the 'doing' words in the creation account. Between the creature and the Creator yawns the outback, infinite in breadth. There is no way you may come upon him in a quiet stroll in a forest. He must always come upon you.

He has done that in the Word: written,

spoken, eaten in Holy Communion, lived in Jesus Christ. That is the beginning of that relationship we call prayer: a person, having heard the breath of God on his ear, lays his own mouth against the ear of God, and is not afraid.

Aub Podlich

Many people seem to feel that science has somehow made 'religious ideas' untimely or old-fashioned. But I think science has a real surprise for sceptics. Science, for instance, tells us that nothing in nature, not even the tiniest particle, can disappear without trace. Nature does not know extinction. All it knows is transformation.

Now, if God applies this fundamental principle to the most minute and insignificant parts of His universe, doesn't it make sense to assume that He applies it also to the human soul? I think it does. And everything science has taught me – and continues to teach me – strengthens my belief in the continuity of our spiritual experience after death. Nothing disappears without trace.

Wernhen van Braun

It is God's privilege to conceal things and
the king's privilege to discover them.

Proverbs 25:2

*These poems are memories of my childhood
appreciation of poetry and nature; God's
wonderful world.*

HOME-THOUGHTS, FROM ABROAD

Oh, to be in England
Now that April's there,
And whoever wakes in England
Sees, some morning, unaware,
That the lowest boughs and the brushwood sheaf
Round the elm-tree bole are in tiny leaf,
While the chaffinch sings on the orchard bough
In England – now!

And after April, when May follows,
And the whitethroat builds, and all the swallows –
Hark! where my blossomed pear-tree in the hedge
Leans to the field and scatters on the clover
Blossoms and dewdrops – at the bent spray's edge –
That's the wise thrush; he sings each song twice over,
Lest you should think he never could recapture
The first fine careless rapture!
And though the fields look rough with hoary dew,
All will be gay when noontide wakes anew

The buttercups, the little children's dower,
– Far brighter than this gaudy melon-flower!

Robert Browning

TO DAFFODILS

Fair Daffodils, we weep to see
You haste away so soon;
As yet the early rising sun
Has not attained his noon.
Stay, stay,
Until the hasting day
Has run
But to the evensong,
And, having prayed together, we
Will go with you along.

We have short time to stay, as you,
We have as short a spring;
As quick a growth to meet decay,
As you, or anything.
We die,
As your hours do, and dry
Away,
Like to the summer's rain;
Or as the pearls of morning's dew,
Ne'er to be found again.

Robert Herrick

LINES WRITTEN IN EARLY SPRING

I heard a thousand blended notes,
While in a grove I sate reclined,
In that sweet mood when pleasant thoughts
Bring sad thoughts to the mind.

To her fair works did nature link
The human soul that through me ran;
And much it grieved my heart to think
What man has made of man.

Through primrose-tufts, in that sweet bower,
The periwinkle trailed its wreathes;
And 'tis my faith that every flower
Enjoys the air it breathes.

The birds around me hopped and played:
Their thoughts I cannot measure,
But the least motion which they made,
It seemed a thrill of pleasure.

The budding twigs spread out their fan,
To catch the breezy air;
And I must think, do all I can,
That there was pleasure there.

If these thoughts may not prevent,
If such be of my creed the plan,
Have I not reason to lament
What man has made of man?

William Wordsworth

Wordsworth was probably the favourite poet of my youth, and although not included in this anthology I recently came across his sister Dorothy's description of the scene which inspired his poem about daffodils, 'I wandered lonely as a cloud'.

DAFFODILS AT GOWBARROW PARK

Thursday, 15 April 1802

It was a threatening, misty morning, but mild. We set off after dinner from Eusemere. Mrs Clarkson went a short way with us but turned back. The wind was furious and we thought we must have turned back. We first rested in the large boathouse, then under a furze bush opposite Mr Clarkson's. Saw the plough going in the field. The wind seized our breath. The lake was rough. There was a boat by itself floating in the middle of the bay below Water Millock. When we were in the woods beyond Gowbarrow Park, we saw a few daffodils close to the waterside. We fancied that the lake had floated the seeds ashore and that the little colony had so sprung up. But as we went along there were more and yet more; and, at last, under the boughs of the trees, we saw that there was a long belt of them along the shore, about the breadth of a country turnpike road.

I never saw daffodils so beautiful. They

grew among the mossy stones, about and about them. Some rested their heads upon these stones, as on a pillow, for weariness; and the rest tossed and reeled and danced, and seemed as if they verily laughed with the wind that blew upon them over the lake. They looked so gay, ever glancing, ever changing. The wind blew directly over the lake to them. There was here and there a little knot, and a few stragglers higher up; but they were so few as not to disturb the simplicity, unity, and life of that one busy highway.

Dorothy Wordsworth

THE SOLITARY REAPER

Behold her, single in the field,
Yon solitary Highland Lass!
reaping and singing by herself;

Stop here, or gently pass!
Alone she cuts and binds the grain,
And sings a melancholy strain;
O listen! for the Vale profound
Is overflowing with the sound.

No Nightingale did ever chaunt
So sweetly to reposing bands
Of Travellers in some shady haunt,
Among Arabian Sands:
No sweeter voice was ever heard
In spring-time from the Cuckoo-bird,
Breaking the silence of the seas
Among the farthest Hebrides.

Will no one tell me what she sings? –
Perhaps the plaintive numbers flow
For old, unhappy, far-off things,
And battles long ago:
Or is it some more humble lay,
Familiar matter of today?
Some natural sorrow, loss or pain,
That has been, and may be again!

Whate'er the theme, the Maiden sang
As if her song could have no ending;
I saw her singing at her work,
And o'er the sickle bending;
I listened till I had my fill:
And, as I mounted up the hill,
The music in my heart I bore,
Long after it was heard no more.

William Wordsworth

TO AUTUMN

Season of mists and mellow fruitfulness,
Close bosom-friend of the maturing sun;
Conspiring with him how to load and bless
With fruit the vines that round the thatch-eaves run;
To bend with apples the moss'd cottage-trees,
And fill all fruit with ripeness to the core;
To swell the gourd, and plump the hazel shells
With a sweet kernel; to set budding more,
And still more, later flowers for the bees,
Until they think warm days will never cease,
For Summer has o'er-brimm'd their clammy cells.

Who hath not seen thee oft amid thy store?
Sometimes whoever seeks abroad may find
Thee sitting careless on a granary floor,
Thy hair soft-lifted by the winnowing wind;
Or on a half-reap'd furrow sound asleep,
Drows'd with the fume of poppies, while thy hook
Spares the next swath and all its twined flowers:
And sometimes like a gleaner thou dost keep
Steady thy laden head across a brook;
Or by a cider-press, with patient look,
Thou watchest the last oozings, hours by hours.

Where are the songs of Spring? Ay, where are they?
Think not of them, thou hast thy music too, –
While barred clouds bloom the soft-dying day,
And touch the stubble-plains with rosy hue;
Then in a wailful choir the small gnats mourn
Among the river sallows, borne aloft
Or sinking as the light wind lives or dies;

And full-grown lambs loud bleat from hilly bourn;
Hedge-crickets sing; and now with treble soft
The red-breast whistles from a garden croft;
And gathering swallows twitter in the skies.

John Keats

Every year after the long strain of winter our
whole being begins to ache for all that the
summer means. Quiet Sunday afternoons, for
instance, with a book on a secluded lawn, the
shadow of beeches on the grass, and the
clouds floating slowly across the blue above
our heads, the silence refined rather than
broken by the occasional hum of a bee passing
from flower to flower. 'Like a walled-in garden
to a troubled mind.' What a description of the
peace of God! I know some gardens that seem
to have about them a secret peace in which the
whole personality seems bathed and restored.

Leslie D. Weatherhead

SEPTEMBER

Now every day the bracken browner grows,
Even the purple stars
Of clematis, that shone about the bars,
Grow browner; and the little autumn rose
Dons, for her rosy gown,
Sad weeds of brown.

Now falls the eve; and ere the morning sun,
Many a flower her sweet life will have lost,
Slain by the bitter frost,
Who slays the butterflies also, one by one,
The tiny beasts
That go about their business and their feasts.

Mary Coleridge

NO!

No sun – no moon!
No morn – no noon –
No dawn – no dusk – no proper time of day –
No sky – no earthly view –
No distance looking blue –
No road – no street – no 't' other side the way –
No end to any Row –
No indications where the Crescents go –
No top to any steeple –
No recognitions of familiar people –
No courtesies for showing 'em –
No knowing 'em! –
No travelling at all – no locomotion,
No inkling of the way – no notion –
'No go' – by land or ocean –
No mail – no post –
No news from any foreign coast –
No Park – no Ring – no afternoon gentility –
No company – no nobility –

No warmth, no cheerfulness, no healthful ease,
No comfortable feel in any member –
No shade, no shine, no butterflies, no bees,
No fruits, no flowers, no leaves, no birds, –
November!

Thomas Hood

THE LORD CHALLENGES JOB

Then the LORD answered Job from the whirlwind: 'Who is this that questions my wisdom with such ignorant words? Brace yourself, because I have some questions for you, and you must answer them.

'Where were you when I laid the foundations of the earth? Tell me, if you know so much. Do you know how its dimensions were determined and who did the surveying? What supports its foundations, and who laid its cornerstone as the morning stars sang together and all the angels shouted for joy?

'Who defined the boundaries of the sea as it burst from the womb, and as I clothed it with clouds and thick darkness? For I locked it behind barred gates, limiting its shores. I said, "Thus far and no farther will you come. Here your proud waves must stop."

'Have you ever commanded the morning to appear and caused the dawn to rise in the east? Have you ever told the daylight to spread to the ends of the earth, to bring an end to the night's wickedness? For the features of the earth take shape as the light approaches, and the dawn is robed in red. The light disturbs the haunts of the wicked and it stops the arm that is raised in violence.

'Have you explored the springs from which the seas come? Have you walked about and explored their depths? Do you know where the gates of death are located? Have you seen the gates of utter gloom? Do you realize the extent of the earth? Tell me about it if you know!

'Where does the light come from, and where does the darkness go? Can you take it to its home? Do you know how to get there? But of course you know all this! For you were born before it was all created, and you are so very experienced!

'Have you visited the treasuries of the snow? Have you seen where the hail is made and stored? I have reserved it for the time of trouble, for the day of battle and war. Where is the path to the origin of light? Where is the home of the east wind?

'Who created a channel for the torrents of rain? Who laid out the path for the lightning? Who makes the rain fall on barren land, in a desert where no one lives? Who sends the rain that satisfies the parched ground and makes the tender grass spring up?

'Does the rain have a father? Where does dew come from? Who is the mother of the ice? Who gives birth to the frost from the heavens? For the water turns to ice as hard as rock, and the surface of the water freezes.

'Can you hold back the movements of the stars? Are you able to restrain the Pleiades or Orion? Can you ensure the proper sequence of the seasons or guide the constellation of the Bear with her cubs across the heavens? Do you know the laws of the universe and how God rules the earth?

'Can you shout to the clouds and make it rain? Can you make lightning appear and cause it to strike as you direct it? Who gives intuition and instinct? Who is wise enough to count all the clouds? Who can tilt the water jars of heaven, turning the dry dust to clumps of mud?

'Can you stalk prey for a lioness and satisfy
the young lions' appetites as they lie in their
dens or crouch in the thicket? Who provides
food for the ravens when their young cry out
to God as they wander about in hunger?'

THE LORD'S CHALLENGE CONTINUES

'Do you know when the mountain goats
give birth? Have you watched as the wild
deer are born? Do you know how many
months they carry their young? Are you
aware of the time of their delivery? They
crouch down to give birth to their young
and deliver their offspring. Their young
grow up in the open fields, then leave their
parents and never return.'

Job 38–39:4

FACING THE STORM

Lord, I don't know how it is,
but we've turned
the beauty of the world you made
into a desert.
Cut down the forests of your love
with sharpened blades of hate.
Polluted the rivers of your grace
with selfishness.
We've brought division,
built barriers,
marked boundaries.
And from the steps and platforms
of our dogmas,
shouted war.
We've found it easy to destroy,
by indifference as much as evil.
We're learning now
how hard it is
to build and re-create.

And yet you love us.
Can love be so elastic
that it stretches out and out
to take in all we've done
and still forgive?
You tell us so.
And show it in torn hands,
marked hard by crucifixion.

Lord, stand with us at the barricades.
And help us, not to fight,
but to dismantle them.
Help us to open up
the road to reconciliation.
To plant and water seeds of trust.
To reach out hands of love,
take partners,
dance forgiveness.

Eddie Askew

CHAPTER THREE

And I think to myself ...

❊ ❊ ❊

For the LORD your God is bringing you into a good land, with springs and underground waters welling up in valleys and hills, a land of wheat and barley, of vines and fig trees and pomegranates, a land of olive trees and honey.

Deuteronomy 8:7–8

CELEBRATION

Deuteronomy

As God has led, protected, and provided for you, celebrate him! As he has helped you become who you are and accomplish what you have done, celebrate him! We celebrate God in our blessings because we acknowledge that it is God from whom those blessings come. When you have a reason to celebrate – a wedding, a new baby, a new job or a promotion, a new home, making it through a rough time, or whatever reason – rejoice, and do so with thanksgiving. Thanksgiving should be at the heart of our celebration, otherwise it is empty partying. Our celebrations should stand for something. Then the joy from them will last long after the actual celebration is over.

Comment from NLT Touchpoint Bible

A PSALM OF THANKSGIVING

Shout with joy to the LORD, O earth!
Worship the LORD with gladness.
Come before him, singing with joy.
Acknowledge that the LORD is God!
He made us, and we are his.
We are his people, the sheep of his pasture.

Enter his gates with thanksgiving;
go into his courts with praise.
Give thanks to him and bless his name.
For the LORD is good.
His unfailing love continues forever,
and his faithfulness continues to each generation.

Psalm 100

Thank you for the music, the songs I'm singing
Thanks for all the joy they're bringing
Who can live without it, I ask in all honesty.
What would life be?
Without a song or a dance, what are we?
So I say thank you for the music, for giving it to me.

Abba

TEACH ME TO DANCE

(Chorus)
Teach me to dance to the beat of your heart,
teach me to move in the pow'r of your Spirit,
teach me to walk in the light of your presence,
teach me to dance to the beat of your heart.
Teach me to love with your heart of compassion,
teach me to trust in the word of your promise,
teach me to hope in the day of your coming,
teach me to dance to the beat of your heart.

You wrote the rhythm of life,
created heaven and earth;
in you is joy without measure.
So, like a child in your sight,
I dance to see your delight,
for I was made for your pleasure – pleasure.

(Chorus)
Teach me to dance ...

Teach me to dance to the beat of your heart.
Teach me to dance to the beat of your heart.

Graham Kendrick

Thank him for all he has done.

Philippians 4:6

We all have experienced those special events
in our lives which are truly memorable. These
have been deeply etched on our minds, and
make us warm and moist-eyed when we recall
them. A particular birthday. A special
experience with another person. A wonderful
holiday. The birth of a child. The list could be
endless.

But our lives are hardly made up of a
continuum of special events. They form the
exception to life which ordinarily is very
pedestrian and prosaic. Much of what we do
is repetitive. And even what might appear to
be exciting to someone else is for us often
lack-lustre. As a consequence, celebration is
hardly the keynote of our lives. It usually only
has the character of the occasional.

Yet it can and should be more central. Being
thankful should undergird all of our lives and
not simply become an expression for that
which is special. We should learn to appreciate
all of life. And this includes light and

shadows, sun and rain, joy and trial. Celebration, similarly, should not occur only at the high points and in the good times. Nouwen reminds us that 'celebration lifts up not only the happy moments, but the sad moments as well'. Celebration is not simply concerned with rejoicing in the good life. It is also concerned with rejoicing in life itself even when it is marked by trial.

Celebration is not simply rejoicing in the gifts we receive; it is also a matter of rejoicing in the Giver even when he comes empty-handed. Celebration affirms our being and not only our well-being. As such it enriches and deepens every part of life.

Charles Ringma

O LORD, our LORD, the majesty of your name fills
    the earth.
Your glory is higher than the heavens
You have taught children and nursing infants to give
    you praise.
They silence your enemies who were seeking revenge.
When I look at the night sky and see the work of
    your fingers –
the moon and the stars you have set in place –
What are the mortals that you should think of us,
    mere humans that you should care for us?
For you made us only a little lower than God, and
    you crowned us with glory and honour.

You put us in charge of everything you made, giving
   us authority over all things –
The sheep and the cattle and all the wild animals,
the birds in the sky, the fish in the sea, and
   everything that swims the ocean currents.
O LORD the majesty of your name fills the earth.

Psalm 8

LEISURE

What is this life if, full of care,
We have no time to stand and stare.

No time to stand beneath the boughs
And stare as long as sheep or cows.

No time to see, when woods we pass,
Where squirrels hide their nuts in grass.

No time to see in broad daylight
Streams full of stars, like skies at night.

No time to turn at Beauty's grace
And watch her feet, how they can dance.

No time to wait till her mouth can
Enrich that smile her eyes began.

A poor life this if, full of care
We have no time to stand and stare.

W. H. Davies

Crown Him with many crowns,
The Lamb upon His Throne:
Hark how the heav'nly anthem drowns –
All music but its own!
Awake, my soul and sing –
Of Him who died for thee,
And hail Him as thy matchless King,
Through all eternity.

Crown Him the Lord of life,
Who triumphed o'er the grave,
And rose victorious in the strife,
For those He came to save:
His glories now we sing,
Who died, and rose on high,
Who died eternal Life to bring,
and lives that death may die.

Crown Him the Lord of peace,
Whose power a sceptre sways
From pole to pole, that wars may cease,
And all be prayer and praise.
All hail! Redeemer, hail!
For Thou hast died for me;
Thy praise and glory shall not fail,
Throughout eternity.

Matthew Bridges and Godfrey Thring

O Lord my God! When I in awesome wonder
Consider all the works thy hand hath made;
I see the stars, I hear the mighty thunder,
Thy power throughout the universe displayed:

(*Chorus*)
Then sings my soul, my Saviour God, to thee,
How great thou art! How great thou art!
Then sings my soul, my Saviour God, to thee,
How great thou art! How great thou art!

When through the woods and forest glades I wander,
And hear the birds sing sweetly in the trees;
When I look down from lofty mountain grandeur,
And hear the brook and feel the gentle breeze;

And when I think that God, his Son not sparing,
Sent him to die, I scarce can take it in;
That on the cross, my burden gladly bearing,
He bled and died to take away my sin:

When Christ shall come with shout of acclamation
And take me home, what joy shall fill my heart!
Then shall I bow in humble adoration
And there proclaim: My God, how great thou art!

Russian hymn, translated by Stuart K. Hine

I am grouping these four psalms together. They are all full of breath-taking worship to God for His creation. The footnote in the New Living Translation explains:

> The psalmist speaks of worship as a reverent celebration. We express our devotion to God by singing His praises and celebrating His goodness with shouts of joy. Yet we also kneel in humility and great reverence before the Creator and Ruler of the Universe. The dual focus of celebration and reverence keep our worship from becoming either too restrained or too superficial. Is your own experience of worship marked by both celebration and reverence?

Come, let us sing to the LORD!
Let us give a joyous shout to the rock of our
    salvation.
Let us come before him with thanksgiving.
Let us sing him psalms of praise.
For the LORD is a great God, the great King above all
    gods.
He owns the depths of the earth, and even the
    mightiest mountains are his.
The sea belongs to him, for he made it.
His hands formed the dry land, too.

Come, let us worship and bow down.
Let us kneel before the LORD our maker, for he is
    our God.
We are the people he watches over, the sheep under
    his care.

Oh, that you would listen to his voice today!

Psalm 95

Sing a new song to the LORD!
Let the whole earth sing to the LORD!
Sing to the LORD; bless his name.
Each day proclaim the good news that he saves.
Publish his glorious deeds among the nations.
Tell everyone about the amazing things he does.
Great is the LORD! He is most worthy of praise!
He is to be revered above all the gods.
The gods of other nations are merely idols,
but the LORD made the heavens!
Honour and majesty surround him;
strength and beauty are in his sanctuary.

O nations of the world, recognise the LORD;
recognise that the LORD is glorious and strong.
Give to the LORD the glory he deserves!
Bring your offering and worship the Lord in all his
    holy splendour
Let all the earth tremble before Him
Tell all the nations that the LORD is king.
The world is firmly established and cannot be shaken.
He will judge all peoples fairly.

Let the heavens be glad, and let the earth rejoice!
Let the sea and everything in it shout his praise!
Let the fields and their crops burst forth with joy!
Let the trees of the forest rustle with praise before
    the LORD!
For the LORD is coming!
He is coming to judge the earth.
He will judge the world with righteousness
and all the nations with his truth.

Psalm 96

The LORD is king! Let the earth rejoice!
Let the farthest islands be glad.
Clouds and darkness surround him.
Righteousness and justice are the foundation of his
    throne.
Fire goes forth before him and burns up all his foes.
His lightning flashes out across the world.
The earth sees and trembles.
The mountains melt like wax before the LORD,
before the LORD of all the earth.
The heavens declare his righteousness;
every nation sees his glory.
Those who worship idols are disgraced –
all who brag about their worthless gods –
for every god must bow to him.
Jerusalem has heard and rejoiced,
and all the cities of Judah are glad
because of your justice, LORD!
For you, O LORD, are most high over all the earth;
you are exalted far above all gods.

You who love the LORD, hate evil!
He protects the lives of his godly people
and rescues them from the power of the wicked.
Light shines on the godly,
and joy on those who do right.
May all who are godly be happy in the LORD
and praise his holy name!

Psalm 97

Sing a new song to the LORD,
for he has done wonderful deeds.
He has won a mighty victory
by his power and holiness.
The LORD has announced his victory
and has revealed his righteousness to every nation!
He has remembered his promise to love
and be faithful to Israel.
The whole earth has seen the salvation of our God
Shout to the LORD, all the earth;
break out in praise and sing for joy!
Sing your praise to the LORD with the harp,
with the harp and melodious song,
with trumpets and the sound of the ram's horn.
Make a joyful symphony before the LORD, the King!
Let the sea and everything in it shout his praise!
Let the earth and all living things join in.
Let the rivers clap their hands in glee!
Let the hills sing out their songs of joy before the LORD
For the LORD is coming to judge the earth.
He will judge the world with justice,
and the nations with fairness.

Psalm 98

I asked of life, 'What have you to offer me?'
The answer came, 'What have you to give?'

Anon.

Life is sweet. It offers sunrises, at baby
fists, darting hummingbirds, commitments,
outstretched arms, spring breezes, puppies,
giggles, surprise parties, strawberries,
voices in harmony, dimples, sheets on a
clothesline, curls on little girls,
compliments, fresh-baked bread, red
wagons, great oak trees, whiskered men,
love letters, pink parasols, marching bands,
harvest time, feather pillows, waterfalls,
boys on bikes, praise songs, full moons,
cosy fires, communion, reunions, daisies,
helping hands, pounding surf, butterflies
and white clouds mounded in blue skies.

Life is sharp. It pierces with goodbyes,
fevered brows, screams, empty beds,
tornadoes and earthquakes, prejudice,
poison ivy, traffic jams, tear-stained cheeks,
ignorance, failure, war, drought,
explosions, greed, lies, criticism, head-on
collisions, rust and rot, floods, doubts,
rejection, wrinkles, mosquitoes, hunger,
hands that slap or steal, despair, divorce,
rape, depression, broken bones, broken
promises, broken dreams, broken hearts,
broken lives and dark clouds mounded in
grey skies.

How can we enjoy the sweetness of this life without being pricked by its jagged thorns? How can we feel at home in a world blighted by sin yet blessed with the redeeming grace and presence of God?

God's children are not at home here; but we are here nonetheless. And we discover that it's impossible to enjoy this world's sunshine without enduring its clouds and storms. There is no way to withdraw from only one part of life. Resistance to pain inevitably numbs us to joy.

So we accept the reality that this world of dashing darkness and light is where we are required to live and mature. But for now our job is to stand firm and grow where we are planted by using all the sunshine and rain that comes our way. Would we come to harvest without either?

> What awe
> What wonder,
> for tiny man on
> frail earth
> to realize that
> size
> is
> no measure of
> worth
> in God's enormous eyes.

Susan Lenzkes

Worry does not empty tomorrow of its sorrows, it empties today of its strength.

Corrie ten Boom

WHAT IS LIFE?

Life is a challenge – Meet it
Life is a gift – Accept it

Life is an adventure – Dare it
Life is a sorrow – Overcome it

Life is a tragedy – Face it
Life is a duty – Perform it

Life is a game – Play it
Life is a mystery – Unfold it

Life is a song – Sing it

Life is an opportunity – Take it
Life is a journey – Complete it

Life is a promise – Fulfil it
Life is a love – Enjoy it

Life is a beauty – Praise it
Life is a spirit – Realise it

Life is a struggle – Fight it
Life is a puzzle – Solve it

Life is a goal – Achieve it.

BEGIN TODAY

Dream not too much of what you'll do tomorrow,
How well you'll work another year;
Tomorrow's chance you do not need to borrow –
Today is here.
Boast not too much of mountains you will master
The while you linger in the vale below,
To dream is well, but plodding brings us faster
To where we go.
Talk not too much about some new endeavour
You mean to make a little later on.
Who idles now will idle on forever
'Til life is gone.
Swear not some day to break some habit's fetter,
When this old year is dead and passed away;
If you have need of living wiser, better,
Begin today.

Anon.

Yesterday is past, tomorrow is possible, today is a gift which is why it is called the present.

When Life says to us, 'Enter on a course of work,' it says, 'Enter, and sometimes fail, and live through the failure.' If it says, 'Work and live with other people,' it says, 'Live with, and care for, those who will sometimes hurt you and sometimes be hurt by you; and bear both.' If it says, 'Go and carry out an ideal,' it includes, 'Go and carry it out, often imperfectly; and make mistakes, and have doubts, and take all the pain of this as well as the pain of right doing.'

Helen Wodehouse

God calls us, not to be successful but to be faithful.

Those who bring sunshine into the lives of others cannot keep it from themselves.

J. M. Barrie

I asked God for strength that I might achieve;
I was made weak that I might learn humbly to obey.

I asked for help that I might do greater things;
I was given infirmity that I might do better things.

I asked for riches that I might be happy;
I was given poverty that I might be wise.

I asked for power that I might have the praise of
    others;
I was given weakness that I might feel the need of
    God.

I asked for all things that I might enjoy life;
I was given life that I might enjoy all things.

I got nothing that I asked for – but everything I'd
    hoped for.
My unspoken prayers were answered.
I am among all men most richly blessed!

An unknown nineteenth-century soldier

People say they are tired of life; no man was
ever tired of life; the truth is that we are tired
of being half dead while we are alive. What
we need is to be transfigured by the
incoming of a great and New Life.

Oswald Chambers

Lord, I find it hard to understand,
your emphasis on weak and foolish.
The world just laughs,
and turns its back.
The testing ground
is marketplace and jungle.
The tough survive
in the killing fields of commerce.
The weak go to the wall.
Their epitaphs written in bank balances.
Black or red.

Not very different in your day.
I see you
surrounded by the strong.
Romans, armoured in authority.
Priest, implacable in piety.
Manipulating the gold of betrayal
and taking a profit.
Making a killing, as we say.

Yet when you look beyond the obvious,
the show of strength is flawed.
Vulnerable.
Strength made brittle
by a core of fear.
Hollow men,
their anguish echoing deep within.

I turn to you.
And here I see
no show of strength,
coercing me to faith.
Rather a quiet patience,
loving me to surrender.
Your weakness strengthened
by a core of love,
resilient as life.
Springing renewed from every pruning.
Surviving, growing,
its annual returns
measured in mercy.

Lord if it's the weak you want,
the foolish,
then I'm the one.

Eddie Askew

ENCOUNTERS

Eternal God, you are a song amid silence,
a voice out of quietness,
a light out of darkness,
a Presence in the emptiness, a coming out of the
    void.
You are all these things and more.
You are mystery that encompasses meaning,
meaning that penetrates mystery.

You are God,
I am man.
I strut and brag.
I put down my fellows
and bluster out assertions of my achievements.
And then something happens:
I wonder who I am
and if I matter.
Night falls,
I am alone in the dark and afraid.
Someone dies,
I feel so powerless.
A child is born,
I am touched by the miracle of new life.
At such moments I pause ...
to listen for a song amid silence,
a voice out of stillness,
to look for a light out of darkness.
I want to feel a Presence in the emptiness.
I find myself reaching for a hand.
Oftentimes, the feeling passes quickly,
and I am on the run again:
success to achieve,
money to make.
O Lord, you have to catch me on the run
most of the time.
I am too busy to stop,
too important to pause for contemplation.
I hold up too big a section of the sky
to sit down and meditate.
But even on the run,
an occasional flicker of doubt assails me,
And I suspect I may not be as important

to the world
as I think I am.
Jesus said each of us is important to you.
It is as if every hair of our heads were numbered.
How can that be?
But in the hope that it is so,
I would stop running,
stop shouting,
and be myself.

Let me be still now.
Let me be calm.
Let me rest upon the faith that you are God,
and I need not be afraid.

Kenneth G. Phifer

And He will give you all you need from day
to day if you live for Him and make the
Kingdom of God your primary concern.

Matthew 6:33

LORD, I HAVE TIME

I went out, Lord.
Men were coming out.
They were coming and going, walking and running.
Everything was rushing, cars, lorries, the street, the
    whole town.
Men were rushing not to waste time.
They were rushing after time,
To catch up with time,
To gain time.

Goodbye, sir, excuse me, I haven't time.
I'll come back, I can't wait, I haven't time.
I'd love to help you, but I haven't time.
I can't accept, having no time.
I can't think, I can't read, I'm swamped, I haven't
    time.
I'd like to pray, but I haven't time.

You understand, Lord, they simply haven't the time.

But we must not lose time, waste time, kill time,
For time is a gift that you give us,
But a perishable gift,
A gift that does not keep.

Lord, I have time,
I have plenty of time,
All the time that you give me,
The years of my life,
The days of my years,
The hours of my days,

They are all mine.
Mine to fill, quietly, calmly,
But to fill completely, up to the brim.
To offer them to you, that of their insipid water
You may make a rich wine such as you made once in
    Cana of Galilee.
I am not asking you tonight, Lord,
for time to do this and that,
But your grace to do conscientiously, in time
that you give me, what you want me to do.

Michel Quoist

CHAPTER FOUR

I see skies of blue ...

＊ ＊ ＊

THE ARTIST

I love the way you paint the sky
With autumn's brilliant blues,
And winter's powder grey.
I love the way you pour the ocean out,
And send it shouting to the shore.
I see here how nature's life expresses you.
The rain the storms,
The relentless burning sun.
You must laugh at our God-denial.
We think we're so together, so advanced.
Inventions, conventions, so evolved,
Man on the moon.
But who sets this barren orb into a midnight sky
And keeps it there?
Who summons the dawn without fail,
And gathers up a whispering wind,
That strips the trees of leaves?
Give us eyes that see,
And hearts that are an echo of your own.
That in those dull and shaky moments,

With vision cleared we will read the natural signs of
    you,
God ... our mighty creator.

Tricia Richards

KALEIDOSCOPE

I love the world of sun and rain
I love the hue and cry
Of great white clouds that endless run across the
    open sky
I love the morning's silent gray
And everything's sunset glow
And summer days of shining warmth
And gently falling snow
I love the ever changing world
of sea and sky and ground with light and darkness,
    sun and rain
and silence after sound.

John Harris

SEA FEVER

I must down to the sea again, to the lonely sea and
the sky,
And all I ask is a tall ship and a star to steer her by,
And the wheel's kick and the wind's song and the
white sail's shaking,
And a grey mist on the sea's face and a grey dawn
breaking.

I must down to the sea again, for the call of the
running tide
Is a wild call and a clear call that may not be denied;
And all I ask is a windy day with the white clouds
flying,
And the flung spray and the blown spume, and the
sea-gulls crying.

I must down to the sea again, to the vagrant gypsy
life,
To the gull's way and whale's way where the wind's
like a whetted knife;
And all I ask is a merry yarn from a laughing fellow-
rover,
And quiet sleep and a sweet dream when the long
trick's over.

John Masefield

CHAPTER FIVE

The bright blessed day ...

* * *

Think, every morning when
the sun peeps through
The dim, leaf-latticed
windows of the grove
How jubilant the happy
birds renew their old,
melodious, madrigals of love!
And when you think
of this, remember too
'Tis always morning
somewhere and above
The awakening continents
from shore to shore,
Somewhere the birds
are singing evermore.

Henry Wadsworth Longfellow

COMPOSED UPON WESTMINSTER BRIDGE

Earth has not anything to show more fair:
Dull would he be of soul who could pass by
A sight so touching in its majesty:
This City now doth like a garment wear
The beauty of the morning: silent, bare,
Ships, towers, domes, theatres, and temples lie
Open unto the fields, and to the sky,
All bright and glittering in the smokeless air.

Never did sun more beautifully steep
In his first splendour valley, rock, or hill;
Ne'er saw I, never felt, a calm so deep!
The river glideth at his own sweet will:
Dear God! the very houses seem asleep;
And all that mighty heart is lying still!

William Wordsworth

Lost, yesterday,
somewhere between
sunrise and sunset,
two golden hours,
each set with
sixty diamond minutes.
No reward is offered,
for they are gone forever.

Horace Mann

O SUMMER SUN

O summer sun, O moving trees!
O cheerful human noise, O busy glittering street!
What hour shall Fate in all the future find,
Or what delights, ever to equal these:
Only to taste the warmth, the light, the wind,
Only to be alive, and feel that life is sweet?

Laurence Binyon

CHAPTER SIX

The dark
sacred night ...

✻ ✻ ✻

The night is like a precious gift
When all is blanketed with snow;
It's time for sitting by the fire
And reading in the soft lamp glow.
The world is hushed as nature takes
A quiet rest and winter sleep;
The woodlands dream
their tranquil dreams,
The silvered streams are frozen deep.
The soul refreshes from the calm
When earth is white
and hurries cease;
Contentment spreads
its silken wings;
Hearts find a sweet
accord with peace.

Inez Franck

SONG IN THE NIGHT

Whenever I feel darkness all around,
I can trust that in the dark –
there your light is found.
For in the silent shadows of my heart,
Lord, you shine in and make the music start.

(Chorus)
You are my song in the night,
I speak your name and I am
strong in the night.
I hear your voice, I feel you near
and all I need is here
in the presence of your light,
you are my song in the night.

I'm at peace within your perfect care,
there's no place so deep and dark
that you will not be there.
For I can trust you like the coming dawn,
you pour out the music that plays on and on.

When I feel the peace and joy
your love can bring,
is it any wonder that my heart can sing?

Clair Cloninger and Kathy Frizzell

The evening and the morning were the first day.

Genesis 1:5

How different is God's method from man's! The creature works from day to night, his best is first; but darkness overshadows his fairest hopes and best-concerted schemes. The Creator's days begin with the preceding eve. He reckons the evenings and nights into the days, because out of them the day is born; they usher in the light, and recreate body and brain for the busy hours that follow.

Art thou disappointed in Christian work? Remember that God wrought on through long dark ages ere His schemes were evolved in order and beauty. Human schemes begin with blare of trumpet and roll of drum, but are soon plunged in darkness. The heavenly seed is sown in autumn shadows; the foundation-stone of redemption was laid amid the gloom of Calvary; the work that lasts generally begins amid disappointment, difficulty and heart-break, but inevitably passes into day.

Art thou passing through the bitterness of soul-trouble? For weeks there has been no ray of comfort, no sign of deliverance. Yet every dark hour is hasting towards the dawn. Thou shalt see Thy Beloved walking towards thee in the morning light.

Art thou in despair for the world? The times are dark, and threaten to get darker. But if the first creation began in the dark, can it be wondered at that the second must begin there too? But as the one emerged in daylight, so shall the other. The morning cometh; see the start of day standing sentry! Time is bearing us to a day that shall never go down to night, but shall mount ever towards its meridian.

F. B. Meyer

Glory to Thee, my God, this night
For all the blessings of the light;
Keep me, O keep me, King of kings,
Beneath Thine own almighty wings.

Forgive me, Lord, for Thy dear Son,
The ill that I this day have done,
That with the world, myself, and Thee,
I, ere I sleep, at peace may be.

Teach me to live – that I may dread –
The grave as little as my bed;
Teach me to die – that so I may –
Rise glorious at the aweful day.

O may my soul on Thee repose
And may sweet sleep mine eyelids close,
Sleep that shall me more vigorous make
To serve my God when I awake.

Praise God, from Whom all blessings flow;
Praise Him, all creatures here below;
Praise Him above, ye heav'nly host;
Praise Father, Son, and Holy Ghost.

Thomas Ken

Lord, there are times
when I'm tempted to give up.
When all the pressures of my world,
darken my vision,
wear down my will.
And, footweary and head low,
I find it all a burden hard to bear.
Standing against the powers of the age
seems futile.
Don Quixote without a donkey.

My world looks dark,
my faith a dusty relic
seen dimly through the smeared glass
of a museum showcase,
long unvisited.
The fossil bones of faith dust covered.
A prehistoric curiosity.
Hard to believe those bones
were once the stuff of life.

And yet, within the dark,
the candles glow.
Frail flames of flickering light.
Will-o'-the-wisps of faith,
now here, now there,
but leading to fulfilment.
As one seems quenched
another glows,
sparks into light.
Darkness is distanced,
and, in light's small flame,
hope warms its hands.
And I am strengthened to renew my trust
in love, alive and well.
In time,
in God's own time,
the flames will grow
and coalesce into a dawn
when earth is filled with light
from end to end.

Meanwhile, Lord, I'll gather up my courage
for one more day.

Eddie Askew

THE MOON IS UP

The moon is up: the stars are bright:
The wind is fresh and free!
We're out to seek for gold to-night
Across the silver sea!
The world was growing grey and old:
Break out the sails again!
We're out to seek a Realm of Gold
Beyond the Spanish Main.

We're sick of all the cringing knees,
The courtly smiles and lies!
God, let Thy singing Channel breeze
Lighten our hearts and eyes!
Let love no more be bought and sold
For earthly loss or gain;
We're out to seek an Age of Gold
Beyond the Spanish Main.

Beyond the light of far Cathay,
Beyond all mortal dreams,
Beyond the reach of night and day
Our El Dorado gleams,
Revealing – as the skies unfold –
A star without a stain,
The Glory of the Gates of Gold
Beyond the Spanish Main.

Alfred Noyes

I will now lay me down and sleep, for thou
LORD only, makest me dwell in safety.

Psalm 2:11

The day Thou gavest, Lord, is ended,
The darkness falls at Thy behest;
To Thee our morning hymns ascended,
Thy praise shall hallow now our rest.

We thank Thee that Thy church unsleeping,
While earth rolls onward into light,
Through all the world her watch is keeping,
And rests not now by day or night.

As o'er each continent and island,
The dawn leads on another day,
The voice of prayer is never silent,
Nor dies the strain of praise away.

The sun – that bids us rest – is waking
Our brethren 'neath the western sky,
And hour by hour fresh lips are making
Thy wondrous doings heard on high.

So be it, Lord – Thy throne shall never,
Like earth's proud empires, pass away,
Thy Kingdom stands and grows for ever,
Till all Thy creatures own Thy sway.

John Ellerton

A NIGHT-PIECE

The sky is overspread
With a close veil of one continuous cloud
All whitened by the moon, that just appears,
A dim-seen orb, yet chequers not the ground
With any shadow – plant, or tower, or tree.
At last a pleasant instantaneous light
Startles the musing man whose eyes are bent
To earth. He looks around, the clouds are split
Asunder, and above his head he views
The clear moon and the glory of the heavens.
There in a black-blue vault she sails along
Followed by multitudes of stars, that small,
And bright, and sharp along the gloomy vault
Drive as she drives. How fast they wheel away!
Yet vanish not! The wind is in the trees;
But they are silent. Still they roll along
Immeasurably distant, and the vault
Built round by those white clouds, enormous clouds,
Still deepens its interminable depth.
At length the vision closes, and the mind
Not undisturbed by the deep joy it feels,
Which slowly settles into peaceful calm,
Is left to muse upon the solemn scene.

Anon.

*T*his is a hymn I have loved since childhood. It is well-known now and sung by many people at football matches, who would not even believe what they are singing. But the words are so powerful and victorious that I never fail to have goose-bumps as I sing them.

Abide with me, fast falls the eventide;
The darkness deepens; Lord, with me abide:
When other helpers fail, and comforts flee,
Help of the helpless, O abide with me.

Swift to its close ebbs out life's little day;
Earth's joys grow dim, its glories pass away;
Change and decay in all around I see;
O thou who changest not, abide with me.

I need thy presence ev'ry passing hour;
What but thy grace can foil the tempter's pow'r?
Who like thyself my guide and stay can be?
Through cloud and sunshine, Lord, abide with me.

I fear no foe with thee at hand to bless;
Ills have no weight, and tears no bitterness.
Where is death's sting? Where, grave, thy victory?
I triumph still, if thou abide with me.

Hold thou thy cross before my closing eyes;
Shine through the gloom, and point me to the skies;
Heav'n's morning breaks, and earth's vain shadows
    flee;
In life, in death, O Lord, abide with me.

Henry Francis Lyte

NIGHT OF NIGHTS

Now it is night. But it is to become the greatest, most significant night of history. It is the night that will conquer darkness and bring in the day when there shall be night no more. It is the night when those who sit in darkness shall see a great light. It is the night that shall make eternal light, for it is the night when God shall bring into the world him who is the light of the world.

In the stable of the inn at Bethlehem, where the cattle are breathing softly in slumber, a virgin mother brings forth her child and lays him in a manger. Over the cave a bright star shines and an angelic chorus begins to sing. What a moment! What an hour! This is Emmanuel, God with us. It staggers our imagination to believe that God himself has become a man in the person of his Son.

The incarnation of Jesus Christ is not merely a doctrinal tenet about which theologians of different schools may hold differing views. It is a glorious reality, a wondrous fact apart from which there can be no salvation for sinful men. Who in the world that Rome ruled at the time could possibly believe that this little baby in a stable was the great God of creation come in the flesh? This child nestled in Mary's arms would be both God and man united in one person, never again to be separated. This is the glorious mystery of the incarnation ...

Who would dream that he is the King of kings and Lord of lords? Who would imagine in Rome that night that he would reach down the ages, overturning kingdoms and empires, changing the world; and that even today, two thousand years later, millions would be ready to die for him?

Billy Graham

I have had the privilege of meeting Dr Graham (and even speaking on the same platform at one of his meetings). I have admired him from near and afar and this excerpt from a book, Billy Graham in Conversation with David Frost, *is I think an accurate description of an amazing man.*

Frost: What would you like the first line of your obituary to say?

Graham: Well, I suppose that 'He was faithful,' and that 'He had integrity.' Because the psalmist said, 'I walk in my integrity,' and I would like to be considered a person who had integrity, and who was faithful to his calling, and who loved God with all his heart, mind, and soul.

Frost: You're obviously going to heaven, aren't you?

Graham: Well, I'm going to heaven, not on my good works, or because I've preached to all these people or read the Bible. I'm going to heaven because of what Christ did on the cross.

Frost: I hope this is not our last interview. But, if this were to be our last interview, what is the message you would most want to communicate at the end of it?

Graham: That God loves you. I tell people in every crusade we hold, 'If you forget everything that happens in this crusade, remember one thing, God loves you.' Because God does love you. No matter what you've done or what you've said or been, he loves you. And that love is impossible for us to describe, because he uses totally different terminology to describe it in the Greek language, to describe God's love. And then when God's love comes into our hearts, that too is supernatural. There are some people that maybe you wouldn't normally love, but he gives you the power to love that person. And I can say to you right now, that I just – I love everybody. I don't have any people I don't like or dislike. I just accept everybody.

. . . *And I think to myself, what a wonderful world ...*

CHAPTER SEVEN

The colours of the rainbow ...

* * *

My heart leaps up when I behold
A rainbow in the sky;
So was it when my life began;
So it is now I am a man;
So be it when I shall grow old,
Or let me die.
The child is a father of the man
And I could wish my days to be
Bound each to each by natural piety.

William Wordsworth

*T*his delightful song about the rainbow came from the musical Billy which starred Michael Crawford. My husband took over from him for the final months of the run at the famous Theatre Royal, Drury Lane – an opportunity he relished and an ambition fulfilled!

I missed the last rainbow, there's not one in sight
It's hard to find rainbows at this time of night.
I missed the last rainbow, I got here too late
And in between rainbows there's such a long wait.

My fault I know, why am I always so slow?
I've such a long way to go, I should be gone.
If I'm to find the world I see in my mind
Then for the sake of mankind, I'll rainbow on.
I know that
I missed the last rainbow but what if I'm wrong?
What if that same rainbow stops further along?
And if there's a rainbow and I'm sure there's one
I'll get on that rainbow, but I'll have to run.

'If happy little bluebirds fly beyond the rainbow
Why oh why can't I?'

CHAPTER EIGHT

Are also on the faces ...

* * *

Worry weighs a person down, an encouraging word cheers a person up.

Proverbs 12:25

I love to 'people watch' on trains or when I'm waiting for a friend or an appointment. I try to build up a picture of where they've come from, what they do for a living and so on. You can tell a great deal from a person's face in repose. When people look miserable I remember that even if we know people really well, there is always at least one sad factor about a person about which we know nothing. They could be in pain. There's always a possibility that they fought for our freedom in the Second World War and are still nursing the scars. God tells us not to judge and He knows best!

I remember my mother when I was a child saying, 'You look worried!' or 'You're frowning – clear your face!' Apparently a smile is the only facial expression that relaxes the muscles in the face and releases tension. If smiling is good for us, we ought to do more of it.

A merry heart doeth good like medicine.

Proverbs 17:22

We were filled with laughter and we sang for joy.

Psalm 126:2

A poet called Ella Wheeler Wilcox wrote the famous lines:'Laugh and the world laughs with you, weep and you weep alone.' The 'wonderful world' would be less wonderful without the gift of laughter and so I have included some humorous poems which I have enjoyed from childhood.

I have a lovely card which says on the front, 'Don't take life so seriously ...' and on the inside, 'It isn't permanent.' I think that sometimes we take ourselves too seriously and it was a strange contradiction that during the most serious time, when my husband was dying of cancer, we laughed more than at any other time of our lives. We were able to see the funny side of an awful situation.

Here's a prayer which I found in Sir Harry Secombe's autobiography Strawberries and Cream.

THE CLOWN'S PRAYER

Dear Lord, I thank you for calling me to share with others your precious gift of laughter.

May I never forget that it is your gift and my privilege.

As your children are rebuked in their self-importance and cheered in their sadness, let me remember that your foolishness is wiser than man's wisdom.

I am including the following song because it will evoke happy memories for anyone who has been alive during the past forty years. Eric Morecambe was a friend of ours during all that time. He and Ernie Wise were heading the bill with Harry Secombe in a pantomime at the Coventry Hippodrome. I had just left school and was dancing in the chorus! Little did I know at that time that Eric would be instrumental in shaping my destiny, by introducing me to the man I would marry.

Bring me sunshine in your smile
Bring me laughter all the while
In this world I confess there should be more
    happiness
So much joy there should be for each brand new
    bright tomorrow
Make me happy through the years
Never bring me any tears.
Let your arms be as warm as the sun from up above
Bring me fun, bring me sunshine, bring me love.

I grew up with the following poems, and loved them. Although the humour may seem slightly dated in this age of alternative comedy I hope you will agree that the words are brilliantly composed.

STATELY AS A GALLEON

My neighbour, Mrs Fanshaw, is portly-plump and
    gay,
She must be over sixty-seven, if she is a day
You might have thought her life was dull,
It's one long whirl instead.
I asked her all about it, and this is what she said:

I've joined an Olde Thyme Dance club, the trouble
    is that there
Are too many ladies over, and no gentlemen to spare.
It seems a shame, it's not the same,
But still it has to be,
Some ladies have to dance together,
One of them is me.

Stately as a galleon, I sail across the floor,
Doing the Military Two-step, as in the days of yore.
I dance with Mrs Tiverton; she's light on her feet, in
    spite
Of turning the scale at fourteen stone, and being of
    medium height.

So gay the band,
So giddy the sight,
Full evening dress is a must,
But the zest goes out of a beautiful waltz
When you dance it bust to bust.

So, stately as two galleons, we sail across the floor,
doing the Valse Valeta as in the days of yore.
The gent is Mrs Tiverton, I am her lady fair,
She bows to me ever so nicely and I curtsey to her
    with care.
So gay the band,
So giddy the sight,
But it's not the same in the end
For a lady is never a gentleman, though
She may be your bosom friend.

So, stately as a galleon, I sail across the floor,
Doing the dear old Lancers, as in the days of yore.
I'm led by Mrs Tiverton, she swings me round and
    round
And though she manoeuvres me wonderfully well
I never get off the ground.
So gay the band,
So giddy the sight,
I try not to get depressed.
And it's done me a power of good to explode,
and get this lot off my chest.

Joyce Grenfell

A SUBALTERN'S LOVE-SONG

Miss J. Hunter Dunn, Miss J. Hunter Dunn,
Furnish'd and burnish'd by Aldershot sun,
What strenuous singles we played after tea,
We in the tournament – you against me!

Love-thirty, love-forty, oh! weakness of joy,
The speed of a swallow, the grace of a boy,
With carefullest carelessness, gaily you won,
I am weak from your loveliness, Joan Hunter Dunn.

Miss Joan Hunter Dunn, Miss Joan Hunter Dunn,
How mad I am, sad I am, glad that you won.
The warm-handled racket is back in its press,
But my shock-headed victor, she loves me no less.

Her father's euonymus shines as we walk,
And swing past the summer-house, buried in talk,
And cool the verandah that welcomes us in
To the six-o'clock news and a lime-juice and gin.

The scent of the conifers, sound of the bath,
The view from my bedroom of moss-dappled path,
As I struggle with double-end evening tie,
For we dance at the Golf Club, my victor and I.

On the floor of her bedroom lie blazer and shorts
And the cream-coloured walls are be-trophied with
    sports,
And westering, questioning settles the sun

On your low-leaded window, Miss Joan Hunter
    Dunn.
The Hillman is waiting, the light's in the hall,
The pictures of Egypt are bright on the wall,
My sweet, I am standing beside the oak stair
And there on the landing the light's on your hair.

By roads 'not adopted', by woodlanded ways,
She drove to the club in the late summer haze,
Into nine-o'clock Camberley, heavy with bells
And mushroomy, pine-woody, evergreen smells.

Miss Joan Hunter Dunn, Miss Joan Hunter Dunn,
I can hear from the car-park the dance has begun.
Oh! full Surrey twilight! importunate band!
Oh! strongly adorable tennis-girl's hand!

Around us are Rovers and Austins afar,
Above us, the intimate roof of the car,
And here on my right is the girl of my choice,
With the tilt of her nose and the chime of her voice,

And the scent of her wrap, and the words never said,
And the ominous, ominous dancing ahead.
We sat in the car-park till twenty to one
And now I'm engaged to Miss Joan Hunter Dunn.

John Betjeman

MAD DOGS AND ENGLISHMEN

In tropical climes there are certain times of day,
When all the citizens retire
To tear their clothes off and perspire.
It's one of those rules that the greatest fools obey,
Because the sun is much too sultry
And one must avoid its ultry-violet ray ...
The natives grieve when the white men leave their
    huts,
Because they're obviously definitely nuts!

Mad dogs and Englishmen
Go out in the midday sun.
The Japanese don't care to,
The Chinese wouldn't dare to,
The Hindus and Argentines sleep firmly from twelve
    to one,
But Englishmen detest a siesta.
In the Philippines there are lovely screens
To protect you from the glare;
In the Malay States, they have hats like plates
Which the Britishers won't wear.
At twelve noon, the natives swoon,
And no further work is done;
But mad dogs and Englishmen go out in the midday
    sun.

It's such a surprise for the Eastern eyes to see,
That though the English are effete
They're quite impervious to heat.
When the white man rides every native hides in glee,
Because the simple creatures hope he
Will impale his solar topee on a tree …
It seems such a shame when the English claim the
    earth
That they give rise to such hilarity and mirth.

Mad dogs and Englishmen
Go out in the midday sun.
The toughest Burmese bandit
Can never understand it.
In Rangoon the heat of noon is just what the natives
    shun.
They put their Scotch or rye down and lie down.
In a jungle town where the sun beats down
To the rage of man and beast,
The English garb of the English sahib
Merely gets a bit more creased.
In Bangkok at twelve o'clock
They foam at the mouth and run,
But mad dogs and Englishmen go out in the midday
    sun.

Noel Coward

LAUGH AND BE MERRY

Laugh and be merry, remember, better the world
    with a song,
Better the world with a blow in the teeth of a wrong.
Laugh, for the time brief, a thread the length of a
    span.
Laugh, and be proud to belong to the old proud
    pageant of man.

Laugh and be merry: remember in olden time,
God made Heaven and Earth for joy He took in a
    rhyme,
Made them, and filled them full with the strong red
    wine of His mirth,
The splendid joy of the stars: the joy of the earth.

So we must laugh and drink from the deep blue cup
    of the sky,
Join the jubilant song of the great stars sweeping by,
Laugh, and battle, and work, and drink of the wine
    outpoured
In the dear green earth, the sign of the joy of the
    Lord.

Laugh and be merry together, like brothers akin,
Guesting awhile in the rooms of a beautiful inn,
Glad till the dancing stops, and the lilt of the music
    ends.
Laugh till the game is played; and be you merry, my
    friends.

John Masefield

THE LION AND ALBERT

There's a famous seaside place called Blackpool,
That's noted for fresh air and fun,
And Mr and Mrs Ramsbottom
Went there with young Albert, their son.

A grand little lad was young Albert,
All dressed in his best; quite a swell
With a stick with an 'orse's 'ead 'andle,
The finest that Woolworth's could sell.

They didn't think much to the Ocean:
The waves, they was fiddlin' and small,
There was no wrecks and nobody drownded,
Fact, nothing to laugh at at all.

So, seeking for further amusement,
They paid and went into the Zoo,
Where they'd Lions and Tigers and Camels,
And old ale and sandwiches too.

There were one great big Lion called Wallace;
His nose were all covered with scars –
He lay in a somnolent posture,
With the side of his face on the bars.

Now Albert had heard about Lions,
How they was ferocious and wild –
To see Wallace lying so peaceful,
Well, it didn't seem right to the child.

So straightway the brave little feller,
Not showing a morsel of fear,
Took his stick with its 'orse's 'ead 'andle
And pushed it in Wallace's ear.

You could see that the Lion didn't like it,
For giving a kind of a roll,
He pulled Albert inside the cage with 'im,
And swallowed the little lad 'ole.

Then Pa, who had seen the occurrence,
And didn't know what to do next,
Said 'Mother! Yon Lion's 'et Albert',
And Mother said 'Well I am vexed!'

Then Mr and Mrs Ramsbottom –
Quite rightly, when all's said and done –
Complained to the Animal Keeper,
That the Lion had eaten their son.

The keeper was quite nice about it;
He said 'What a nasty mishap.
Are you sure that it's *your* boy he's eaten?'
Pa said 'Am I sure? There's his cap!'

The manager had to be sent for.
He came and he said 'What's to do?'
Pa said 'Yon Lion's 'et Albert,
And 'im in his Sunday clothes, too.'

Then Mother said, 'Right's right, young feller;
I think it's a shame and a sin,
For a lion to go and eat Albert,
And after we've paid to come in.'

The manager wanted no trouble,
He took out his purse right away,
Saying 'How much to settle the matter?'
And Pa said 'What do you usually pay?'

But Mother had turned a bit awkward
When she thought where her Albert had gone.
She said 'No! someone's got to be summonsed' –
So that was decided upon.

Then off they went to the P'lice Station,
In front of the Magistrate chap;
They told 'im what happened to Albert,
And proved it by showing his cap.

The Magistrate gave his opinion
That no one was really to blame
And he said that he hoped the Ramsbottoms
Would have further sons to their name.

At that Mother got proper blazing
'And thank you, sir, kindly,' said she.
'What! Waste all our lives raising children
To feed ruddy Lions? Not me!'

Marriott Edgar

WHAT FOR!

One more word, said my dad,
And I'll give you what for.
What for? I said.
That's right, he said, what for!
No, I said, I mean what for?
what will you give me what for for?
Never you mind, he said. Wait and see.
But what is what for for? he said,
It's to teach you what's what,
That's what.
What's that? I said.
Right, he said, you're for it,
I'm going to let you have it.
Have what? I said.
Have what? he said,
What for, that's what.
Do you want me to really give you
Something to think about?
I don't know, I said,
I'm thinking about it.
Then he clipped me over the ear.
It was the first time he'd made sense
All day.

Noel Petty

LETTER FROM A GIRL TO HER AUNT
TELLING OF A REMARKABLE EXPERIENCE
AT A DINNER PARTY

I went to dinner with a very shy young man – rather pretty he was, with a fair moustache. I made a very bad beginning because I took hold of the back of my chair and the top came off in my hand just as Mr Smith was beginning to say grace, and it so upset me that I dropped my roll straight into my soup with a splash. Then I couldn't make out the young man at all. He talked a great deal of slang but he didn't seem to want to take a ticket for our café chantant and he said he never danced, but I never thought he was a parson because of his ordinary evening dress and his moustache.

Then a terrible drama began. We were eating mince-pies and I suddenly looked and beheld Daddy tethered by a string leading from his mouth to the middle of the table. A bit of the table centre had frayed, a string had crossed his plate and Daddy had eaten the end with his mince-pie. I felt the shy young man was talking to me but I never heard a word he said, and I caught Mum's eye who was opposite. She saw it too and began to grow redder and redder ...

Daddy in blissful ignorance was talking blithely to his neighbour and chewing mince-pie and string. Then he moved his head and the string caught the wine-glasses.

They wobbled about; he looked rather worried – put them straight – and then of course they wobbled again. At last he began to think something was going wrong so he put a large piece of mince-pie out of his mouth and on to his plate and all was well. Then the maid took Daddy's plate away and the portion of mince-pie remained behind! It sat on the table in front of him. Mum and I were going through gymnastic feats to keep our faces straight. She was simply red in the face and the tears began to run down my cheeks. Then my dear Papa, still being blind to the awful situation, knocked the piece of mince-pie off the table on to his knee, thereby pulling the string so that a portion of the table centre jumped forward and the glasses hopped about. Then he continued his conversation and Mum and I were just beginning to calm down a bit when he suddenly pushed the table centre back and up flew the bit of mince-pie off his knee on to the table with a wild hop that nearly finished Mum and me off …

Finally I believe he cut the string but before that happened I was roused by the shy young man repeating over and over again: 'I don't know why you should laugh, I am sure. I shouldn't say I was a curate if I wasn't. I don't see why it's so funny.' All the time he was explaining that he was a curate at St Thomas's I never heard a word. I was reduced to mopping my tears with my dinner-napkin and giving dreadful and unexpected gurgles and the more I tried to explain that I wasn't laughing at him the more certain he got that I was – so it never got settled at all. And Daddy never knew till we told him all about it driving home.

The following piece became a classic in the 1960s when the American comedian Bob Newhart made his album which included this monologue and the famous one concerning the 'driving instructor'.

INTRODUCING TOBACCO TO CIVILISATION

Milestones are never really recognised right away. It takes fifty or sixty years before people realise what an achievement it is. Like take for instance tobacco and the discovery of tobacco. It was discovered by Sir Walter Raleigh and he sent it over to England from the colonies. It seems to me the uses of tobacco aren't obvious, right off the bat, you know? I imagine a phone conversation between Sir Walter Raleigh and the head of the West Indies Company in England, explaining about this shipment of tobacco that he had just sent over. I think it would go something like this:

'Yeah, who is it? Sir Walter Raleigh from the colonies ... yeah, yeah, put him on, will you? Harry, you want to pick up the extension? It's nutty Walt again ... Hi, Walt baby, how are you, guy? Did we get the what? The boatload of turkeys ... Yeah, they arrived fine, Walt. As a matter of fact they're still here. They're wandering all over London as a matter of fact. See that's an American holiday, Walt.

'But ... what is it this time, Walt, you got another winner for us, do you? Tobacco ... What's tobacco, Walt? ... It's a kind of leaf? And you bought eighty tons of it? Let me get this straight now, Walt, you bought eighty tons of leaves? This, er, may come as kind of a surprise to you, Walt, but come fall in England here, we're up to our ... er ... it isn't that kind of leaf. What is it, a special food of some kind, Walt? Not exactly. It has a lot of different uses ... Like what are some of the uses, Walt? Are you saying snuff, Walt? What's snuff? You take a pinch of tobacco ... and you shove it up your nose? And it makes you sneeze? I imagine it would, Walt, yeah. Gee, Golden Rod seems to do it pretty well over here.

'It has some other uses though. You can chew it ... or put it in a pipe ... or you can shred it up and put it on a piece of paper and roll it up. Don't tell me, Walt, don't tell me ... you stick it in your ear, right, Walt? Or between your lips. Then what do you do,

Walt? You set fire to it, Walt? Then what do you do? You inhale the smoke?! You know, Walt, it seems offhand like you could stand in front of the fireplace and have the same thing going for you, you know.

'You see, Walt, we've been a little worried about you, you know. Ever since you put your cape down over that mud. You see, Walt, I think you're going to have a tough time selling people on sticking burning leaves in their mouth ... It's going very big over there, is it? What's the matter, Walt? You spilt you what ... your coffee? What's coffee, Walt? That's a drink you make out of beans, uh? A lot of people have their coffee after their first cigarette in the morning. Is that what you call burning leaves, Walt? "Cigarettes"?

'I tell you what, Walt. Why don't you send us a boatload of those beans too? If you can talk people into putting burning leaves into their mouths, you've gotta go for those beans, Walt. Right. Listen, Walt. Don't call us, we'll call you.

'Right, Walt. Goodbye.'

MRS REECE LAUGHS

Laughter, with us, is no great undertaking:
A sudden wave that breaks and dies in breaking.
Laughter, with Mrs Reece, is much less simple:
It germinates, it spreads, dimple by dimple,
From small beginnings, things of easy girth,
To formidable redundancies of mirth.
Clusters of subterranean chuckles rise,
And presently the circles of her eyes
Close into slits, and all the woman heaves,
As a great elm with all its mounds of leaves
Wallows before the storm. From hidden sources
A mustering of blind volcanic forces
Takes her and shakes her till she sobs and gapes.
Then all that load of bottled mirth escapes
In one wild crow, a lifting of huge hands
And creaking stays, a visage that expands
In scarlet ridge and furrow. Thence collapse,
A hanging head, a feeble hand that flaps
An apron-end to stir an air and waft
A steaming face ... And Mrs Reece has laughed.

Martin Armstrong

*H*ere's a poem by another Walter Raleigh.

WISHES OF AN ELDERLY MAN, WISHED AT A GARDEN PARTY, JUNE 1914

I wish I loved the Human Race;
I wish I loved its silly face;
I wish I loved the way it walks;
I wish I loved the way it talks;
And when I'm introduced to one
I wish I thought *What Jolly Fun!*

Walter Raleigh

THEN LAUGH

Build for yourself a strong box,
Fashion each part with care;
When it's strong as your hand can make it,
Put all your troubles there;
Hide there all thought of your failures,
And each bitter cup that you quaff;
Lock all your heartaches within it,
Then sit on the lid and laugh.

Tell no one else its contents,
Never its secrets share;
When you've dropped in your care and worry
Keep them forever there;
Hide them from sight completely
That the world will never dream half;
Fasten the strong box securely –
Then sit on the lid and laugh.

Bertha Adams Backus

PROGRESS

In longing to be civilised
The human race has realised
That living must be organised
With thought and labour minimised
With modernised and mechanised
And finally computerised.

Today – or so I am advised –
Computers have economised.
Have memorised and analysed,
Have scrutinised and synchronised,
And soon will have unauthorised,
Our life and work monopolised.

Beware, lest they, uncriticised,
By foolish men are idolised,
Until we are all mesmerised,
And hypnotised and terrorised,
And find that *we* are organised,
Devitalised, dehumanised.

Thus, longing to be civilised,
We'll end up being fossilised.

Anon.

L aughter brings heaven to earth.

CHAPTER NINE

I see friends shaking hands ...

* * *

The glory of friendship
is not the outstretched hand,
nor the kindly smile,
nor the joy of companionship;
it's the spiritual inspiration
that comes to one
when he discovers
that someone else believes in him
and is willing to trust him
with his friendship.

Ralph Waldo Emerson

Fix your thoughts on what is true and
honourable and right. Think about things
that are pure and lovely and admirable.
Think about things that are excellent and
worthy of praise.

Philippians 4:8

APPRECIATION: HAVING EYES TO SEE WHAT WE HAVE BEEN GIVEN

The gentle touch of a friend. The surprise birthday party. An exhilarating mountain climb. A wonderful meal. A quiet walk. A stimulating conversation. The sheer audacity of autumn colours. A mother's care. A mellow sunset. A lover's passion. A moment of solitude. A gripping book. An inspiration. Appropriate timing in doing good. A sense of God's presence. Mad hilarity with friends. A stimulating project. Receiving an unexpected gift. Worship. Play. Prayer. Silence. Work. Love. Peace. Friendship. Family.

As we allow our minds to wander over the many facets of our lives, we cannot but help to be amazed. Here and there are the marks of love, the signs of goodness, the indications of grace. Here and there are the gifts of compassion, the fruit of service, the signs of hope, the blessings undeserved. Henri Nouwen gently reminds us that 'every time we experience real goodness or gentleness we know it is a gift'. He is right.

But we need eyes to see and a heart to appreciate what has been given to us. We can rush past. We can be so bent on wanting more through comparing ourselves with others that we fail to enjoy the good that has already been placed in our hands.

Appreciation cannot be an occasional afterthought. It is a way of life in which the

111

present is celebrated, the giver thanked and where we live with a sense of amazement that so much has been placed in such undeserving hands.

Charles Ringma

'What a friend we have in Jesus …'

The gospel is not at all what we would come up with on our own. I, for one, would expect to honour the virtuous over the profligate. I would expect to have to clean up my act before even applying for an audience with a Holy God. But Jesus told of God ignoring a fancy religious teacher and turning instead to an ordinary sinner who pleads, 'God, have mercy.' Throughout the Bible, in fact, God shows a marked preference for 'real' people over 'good' people. In Jesus' own words, 'There will be more rejoicing in heaven over one sinner who repents than over ninety-nine righteous persons who do not need to repent.'

In one of his last acts before death, Jesus forgave a thief dangling on a cross, knowing full well the thief had converted out of plain fear. That thief would never study the Bible, never attend synagogue or church, and never make amends to all those he had wronged.

He simply said 'Jesus, remember me,' and Jesus promised, 'Today you will be with me in paradise.' It was another shocking reminder that grace does not depend on what we have done for God but rather what God has done for us.

Ask people what they must do to get to heaven and most reply, 'Be good.' Jesus' stories contradict that answer. All we must do is cry, 'Help!' God welcomes home anyone who will have him and, in fact, has made the first move already. Most experts – doctors, lawyers, marriage counsellors – set a high value on themselves and wait for clients to come to them. Not God. As Søren Kierkegaard put it,

> When it is a question of a sinner He does not merely stand still, open his arms and say, 'Come hither'; no, He stands there and waits, as the father of the lost son waited, rather He does not stand and wait, He goes forth to seek, as the shepherd sought the lost sheep, as the woman sought the lost coin. He goes – yet no, He has gone, but infinitely farther than any shepherd or any woman, He went, in sooth, the infinitely long way from being God to becoming man, and that way He went in search of sinners.

Kierkegaard puts his finger on perhaps the most important aspect of Jesus' parables.

They were not merely pleasant stories to hold listeners' attention or literary vessels to hold theological truth. They were, in fact, the template of Jesus' life on earth. He was the shepherd who left the safety of the fold for the dark and dangerous night outside. To his banquets he welcomed tax collectors and reprobates and whores. He came for the sick and not the well, for the unrighteous and not the righteous. And to those who betrayed him – especially the disciples, who forsook him at his time of greatest need – he responded like a lovesick father.

Philip Yancey

Life is mostly froth and bubble
Two things stand like stone
Kindness in another's trouble,
Courage in your own.

Adam Lindsay Garda

WHAT HAVE YOU DONE TODAY?

You say you'll do much in the years to come, but
what have you done today?
You plan to give wealth in a princely sum, but how
much have you given away?
You'll heal broken hearts and dry every tear, bring to
them hope and take away fear;
Carry His Word to those far and near; *but what have
you done today?*

You say you'll be kind – after a while, but what have
you done today?
The lonely and hurting wait for your smile, you
promised to light up their way;
Your aim is to give truth a grander birth and to
steadfast faith a deeper worth,
To carry His love to the ends of the earth, *but what
have you done today?*

You plan to reap much in the by-and-by, but what
have you sown today?
You plan to build mansions up in the sky, but what
have you built today?
It's nice to dream and in visions bask, but here and
now have you done your task?
The only real question that matters, I ask, *is what
have you done today?*

Anon.

Love your neighbour as you love yourself.

Matthew 22:39

No action, whether foul or fair
Is ever done, but it leaves somewhere
A record written by fingers ghostly
As a blessing or a curse, and mostly
In the greater weakness or greater strength
Of the acts which follow it, till at length
The wrongs of ages are redressed
And the justice of God made manifest.

Henry Wadsworth Longfellow

Is there any encouragement from belonging to Christ? Any comfort from His love? Any fellowship together in the spirit? Are your hearts tender and sympathetic? Then make me truly happy by agreeing wholeheartedly with each other, loving one another, and working together with one heart and purpose. Don't be selfish; don't live to make a good impression on others. Be humble, thinking of others as better than yourself. Don't think only about your own affairs, but be interested in others too, and what they are doing.

Philippians 2:1– 4

Oh, the inexpressible comfort
of feeling safe with a person,
having neither to weigh thoughts
nor measure words.
A faithful hand will take
and sift them,
keep what is worth keeping,
and then with the breath
of kindness blow the rest away.

Craik

I'm special because God has loved me,
For he gave the best thing he had to save me;
His own Son, Jesus, crucified to take the blame,
For all the bad things I have done.

Thank you, Jesus, thank you, Lord,
For loving me so much,
I know I don't deserve anything;
Help me feel your love right now
To know deep in my heart
That I'm your special friend.

Graham Kendrick

Does a mother forget her baby
Or a woman the child within her womb?
Yet even if these forget,
I will never forget.
I will not forget
My own.
I have carved you on the palm of my hand.

Isaiah 49:15–16

YOU ARE VERY SPECIAL

In all the world there is nobody, nobody like you. Since the beginning of time there has never been another person like you. Nobody has your smile, your eyes, your hands, your hair. Nobody owns your handwriting, your voice. You're Special. Nobody can paint your brushstrokes. Nobody has your taste for food or music or dance or art. Nobody in the universe sees things as you do.

In all the time there has never been anyone who laughs in exactly your way, and what makes you laugh or cry or think may have a totally different response in another. – So – You're Special. You're different from any other person who has ever lived in the history of the universe. You are the only one in the whole creation who has your particular set of abilities. There is always someone who is better at one thing or another. Every person is your superior in at least one way. Nobody in the universe can reach the quality of the combination of your talents, your feelings. Like a roomful of musical instruments some might excel in one way or another but nobody can match the symphonic sound when all are played together. Your symphony.

Through all eternity no one will ever walk, talk, think or do exactly like you. You're Special. You're rare and in all rarity there is enormous value and because of your great value the need for you to imitate anyone else is absolutely wrong. You're Special and it is no accident you are. Please realise that God made you for a special purpose. He has a job for you to do that nobody else can do as well as you can. Out of the billions of applicants only one is qualified. Only one has the unique and right combination of what it takes and that one is You. You're Special.

Anon.

A Christian is full of love to his neighbour, of universal love; not confined to one sect or party; not restrained to those who agree with him in opinions, in outward modes of worship; or to those who are allied to him by blood or recommended by nearness of place. Neither does he love those only that love him or are endeared to him by intimacy of acquaintance. But his love resembles that of him, whose mercy is over all his works. It soars above all these scanty bounds, embracing neighbours and strangers, friends and enemies.

John Wesley

MY FOREVER FRIEND

Everybody needs a little help sometime
No one stands alone.
Makes no difference if you're just a child like me
Or a king upon a throne.

For there are no exceptions
We all stand in the line
Everybody needs a friend
Let me tell you of mine.

He's my forever friend
My leave-me-never friend
From darkest night to rainbow's end.
He's my forever friend.

Even when I turn away He cares for me
His love no one can shake
Even as I walk away he's by my side
With every breath I take.

And sometimes I forget him
My halo fails to shine
Sometimes I'm not *His* friend
but He is always mine.

He's my forever friend ...

If you still don't know the one I'm talking of –
I think it's time you knew
Long ago and far away upon a cross
My friend died for you.

So if you'd like to meet Him
And don't know what to do
Ask my friend into your heart
And he'll be your friend too.

He's my forever friend.

Charlie Lansborough

CHAPTER TEN

They're really saying
'I love you' ...

❋ ❋ ❋

L *ove that costs nothing is worth nothing.*

SONNET 18

Shall I compare thee to a summer's day?
Thou art more lovely and more temperate:
Rough winds do shake the darling buds of May,
And summer's lease hath all too short a date:
Sometime too hot the eye of heaven shines,
And often is his gold complexion dimm'd;
And every fair from fair sometime declines,
By chance, or nature's changing course, untrimm'd;
But thy eternal summer shall not fade
Nor lose possession of that fair thou ow'st,
Nor shall Death brag thou wand'rest in his shade
When in eternal lines to time thou grow'st:
So long as men can breathe or eyes can see,
So long lives this, and this gives life to thee.

William Shakespeare

The definition of a good lover is to satisfy and be satisfied by one partner all of your life.

How do I love thee? Let me count the ways.
I love thee to the depth and breadth and height
My soul can reach, when feeling out of sight
For the ends of Being and ideal Grace.
I love thee to the level of everyday's
Most quiet need, by sun and candlelight.
I love thee freely, as men strive for Right;
I love thee purely, as they turn from Praise.
I love thee with the passion put to use
In my old griefs, and with my childhood's faith.
I love thee with a love I seemed to lose
With my lost saints, – I love thee with the breath,
Smiles, tears, of all my life! – and, if God choose,
I shall but love thee better after death.

Elizabeth Barrett Browning

I was privileged to be married for thirty-one years to a wonderful man. We once saw the film star, Paul Newman, being asked in an interview on television the secret of his happy marriage. His answer was classic and one which we quoted to each other on many occasions. It kept us on our toes! 'If you get steak at home, why go out for hamburger?'

It is better to live alone in the corner of an attic than with a contentious wife in a lovely home!

Proverbs 21:9

Who can find a virtuous and capable wife? She is worth more than precious rubies. Her husband can trust her and she will greatly enrich his life. She will not hinder him but help him all her life.

Proverbs 31:10–12

When Roy was asked to mention, during his cabarets, a wedding anniversary or an engagement, he would often sing the following song. Romantically, he told me that whenever and wherever he sang it he always sang it to me.

Here's to my lady.
Here's a toast to my lady,
And all that my lady means to me.
Like a hearth in the winter
A breeze in the summer
A spring to remember is she.
Tho' the years may grow colder as people grow
    older
It's shoulder to shoulder we'll be.
So be it sunshine or shady
Here's my love to my lady .
And I pray that she'll always love me.

Anon.

It lost some of its romance, however, when once appearing in Las Vegas he developed water on the knee and a swelling the size of a golf ball appeared. He changed the last line to: 'I pray that she'll always love my knee!'

A happy marriage is the union of two good forgivers.

Ruth Bell Graham

To love you as I love myself is to seek to hear you as I want to be heard and to understand you as I long to be understood.

David Augsburger

Love is a many-splendoured thing
It's the April rose that only grows in the early spring.
Love is nature's way of giving
A reason to be living
That makes a man a king.
Once on a high and windy hill
In the morning mist two lovers kissed
And the world stood still.
Then your fingers touched my silent heart and taught
    it how to sing,
Yes, true love's a many-splendoured thing.

Paul Frances Webster

*T*he best definition of marriage I know comes from Rev. Jim Graham:

Marriage is a life-long commitment to an imperfect person.

Give honour to marriage and be faithful to one another in marriage.

Hebrews 13:4

CHAPTER ELEVEN

I hear babies cry ...

❋ ❋ ❋

Mankind owes to the child the best it has to give.

United Nations Declaration

Teach your children to choose the right path and when they are old they will remain on it.

Proverbs 22:6

THE HEART OF A CHILD

Whatever you write
On the heart of a child,
No water can wash it away.
The sands may be shifted
When billows are wild
And the efforts of time may decay.
Some stories may perish,
Some songs be forgot,
But this engraved record,
Time changes it not.
Whatever you write
In the heart of a child
A story of gladness or care –
That heaven has blessed
Or that earth has defiled,
Will linger unchangeably there.
Who writes it has sealed it
Forever and aye.
He must answer to God
On that great judgment day.

Anon.

The days that make us happy make us wise.

John Masefield

RECIPE FOR PRESERVING CHILDREN

1 grassy field
1 dozen children
several dogs
a few puppies – if available
1 brook
pebbles to decorate

Method

Pour children into field. Add dogs and puppies; allow to mix well. Pour brook over pebbles until slightly frothy. When children are brown cool in a warm bath. Serve with milk and biscuits.

WHAT WE ARE, WE SOW!

Be the kind of person
you want your kids
to become.

Steve Chalke

O LORD, you have examined my heart and know
    everything about me.
You know when I sit down or stand up
You know my every thought when far away.
You chart the path ahead of me and tell me where to
    stop and rest.
Every moment you know where I am.
You know what I am going to say even before I say
    it, LORD.
You both precede and follow me.
You place your hand of blessing on my head.
Such knowledge is too wonderful for me,
too great for me to know!

I can never escape from your spirit!
I can never get away from your presence!
If I go up to heaven, you are there; if I go down to
    the place of the dead, you are there.
If I ride the wings of the morning, if I dwell by the
    farthest oceans,
even there your hand will guide me, and your
    strength will support me.
I could ask the darkness to hide me and the light
    around me to become night –
but even in the darkness I cannot hide from you
To you the night shines as bright as day.
Darkness and light are both alike to you.

You made all the delicate, inner parts of my body
and knit me together in my mother's womb.
Thank you for making me so wonderfully complex!
Your workmanship is marvellous – and how well I
    know it.

You watched me as I was being formed in utter
    seclusion,
as I was woven together in the dark of the womb.
You saw me before I was born.
Every day of my life was recorded in your book.
Every moment was laid out before a single day had
    passed.

How precious are your thoughts about me, O God!
They are innumerable!
I can't even count them; they outnumber the grains
    of sand!
And when I wake up in the morning, you are still
    with me!

O God, if only you would destroy the wicked!
Get out of my life, you murderers!
They blaspheme you; your enemies take your name
    in vain.
O LORD, shouldn't I hate those who hate you?
Shouldn't I despise those who resist you?
Yes, I hate them with complete hatred, for your
    enemies are my enemies.

Search me, O God, and know my heart; test me and
    know my thoughts.
Point out anything in me that offends you, and lead
    me along the path of everlasting life.

Psalm 139

CREATIVITY

A look at human anatomy gives us just a glimpse of God's creative genius. Who could conceive and design the intricacies of the human body, then move into the complexities of the human mind? Who could dream of a being that would be something like god, yet not God, a being who could choose God and walk with him and live with him forever? The next time you wiggle a finger, take a step, have a dream, enjoy a meal, solve a problem, or speak a sentence, take a moment to stand in awe of God and praise him for making us.

Footnote to Psalm 139:13–15
from New Living Bible

Do not confine your children to your own learning for they were born in a different time.

Hebrew proverb

THE GREATEST IN THE KINGDOM

About that time the disciples came to Jesus and asked 'Which of us is greatest in the Kingdom of Heaven?'

Jesus called a small child over to him and

put the child among them. Then he said, 'I assure you, unless you turn from your sins and become as little children, you will never get into the Kingdom of Heaven. Therefore, anyone who becomes as humble as this little child is the greatest in the Kingdom of Heaven. And anyone who welcomes a little child like this on my behalf is welcoming me. But if anyone causes one of these little ones who trusts in me to lose faith, it would be better for that person to be thrown into the sea with a large millstone tied around the neck.

'How terrible it will be for anyone who causes others to sin. Temptation to do wrong is inevitable, but how terrible it will be for the person who does the tempting. So if your hand or foot causes you to sin, cut it off and throw it away. It is better to enter heaven crippled or lame than to be thrown into the unquenchable fire with both of your hands and feet. And if your eye causes you to sin, gouge it out and throw it away. It is better to enter heaven half blind than to have two eyes and be thrown into hell.

'Beware that you don't despise a single one of these little ones. For I tell you that in heaven their angels are always in the presence of my heavenly Father.'

Matthew 18:1–10

CHILDREN

To become a Christian we must first humble ourselves like little children, who demonstrate simple yet unquestioning faith. This kind of faith is an example of the kind of humility that recognises God's loving authority over us. Not only did Jesus use the example of children to teach about faith that pleases God, he voiced severe warning to anyone who caused a child to falter in his or her faith. God is pleased when we nurture and strengthen the faith of a child.

Footnote to Matthew 18:2–6 from New Living Translation Bible

Live so that, when your children think of fairness and integrity, they think of you.

Children spell love T. I. M. E.

Steve Chalke

If a child lives with criticism
He learns to condemn;
If a child lives with hostility
He learns to fight;
If a child lives with ridicule
He learns to be shy;
If a child lives with shame
He learns to be guilty.

If a child lives with tolerance
He learns to be patient;
If a child lives with encouragement
He learns confidence;
If a child lives with praise
He learns to appreciate;
If a child lives with fairness
He learns justice.

If a child lives with security
He learns faith;
If a child lives with approval
He learns to like himself;
If a child lives with acceptance and friendship
He learns to give love to the world.

Anon.

I have found that if you love until it hurts
there is no more hurt, only love.

Mother Teresa

Every child comes into the world with the
message that God does not despair of man.

Rabindranath Tagore

*The following poem was a childhood favourite
which I knew by heart.*

I remember, I remember
The house where I was born,
The little window where the sun
Came peeping in at morn;
He never came a wink too soon
Nor brought too long a day;
But now, I often wish the night
Had borne my breath away.

I remember, I remember
The roses, red and white,
The violets, and the lily-cups –
Those flowers made of light!
The lilacs where the robin built,
And where my brother set
The laburnum on his birthday –
The tree is living yet!

I remember, I remember
Where I was used to swing,
And thought the air must rush as fresh
To swallows on the wing;
My spirit flew in feathers then
That is so heavy now,
And summer pools could hardly cool
The fever on my brow.

I remember, I remember,
The fir trees dark and high;
I used to think their slender tops
Were close against the sky:
It was a childish ignorance,
But now 'tis little joy
To know I'm farther off from heaven
Than when I was a boy.

Thomas Hood

Before I got married I had six theories about
bringing up children. Now I have six
children and no theories.

John Wilmor, Earl of Rochester, 1647–80

There is nothing new under the sun.

Ecclesiastes 1:9

The world is going through troubled times. Today's young people only think of themselves. They've got no respect for parents or old people. They've got no time for rules and regulations. To hear them talk, you'd think they knew everything. And what we think of as wise, they just see as foolish. As for the girls, they don't speak, act or dress with any kind of modesty or feminine grace.

Peter the Monk, 1274 AD

If you can't be a good example to your children, you'll have to be a terrible warning.

Cider with Rosie *is a wonderfully descriptive story about country life in the early part of the twentieth century. Here, Laurie Lee, the author, delightfully describes his first day at school. I'm sure it will evoke memories of your own experiences!*

The morning came, without any warning, when my sisters surrounded me, wrapped me in scarves, tied up my boot-laces, thrust a cap on my head, and stuffed a baked potato in my pocket.

'What's this?' I said.

'You're starting school today.'

'I ain't. I'm stopping 'ome.'

'Now, come on, Loll. You're a big boy now.'

'I ain't.'

'You are.'

'Boo-hoo.'

They picked me up bodily, kicking and bawling, and carried me up to the road.

'Boys who don't go to school get put into boxes, and turn into rabbits, and get chopped up Sundays.'

I felt this was overdoing it rather, but I said no more after that. I arrived at the school just three feet tall and fatly wrapped in my scarves. The playground roared like a rodeo, and the potato burned through my thigh. Old boots, ragged stockings, torn trousers and skirts, went skating and skidding around me. The rabble closed in; I was encircled; grit flew in my face like shrapnel. Tall girls with frizzled hair, and huge boys with sharp elbows, began to prod me with hideous interest. They plucked at my scarves, spun me round like a top, screwed my nose and stole my potato.

I was rescued at last by a gracious lady – the sixteen-year-old junior-teacher – who boxed a few ears and dried my face and led me off to The Infants. I spent that first day picking holes in paper, then went home in a smouldering temper.

'What's the matter, Loll? Didn't he like it at school, then?'

'They never gave me the present!'

'Present? What present?'

'They said they'd give me a present.'

'Well, now, I'm sure they didn't.'

'They did! They said: "You're Laurie Lee, ain't you? Well, just you sit there for the present." I sat there all day but I never got it. I ain't going back there again!'

I've included the following letter written to supporters of Care for the Family from Rob Parsons, the organisation's director, because it had a profound effect on me.

We live in a world driven by the desire to succeed, and this letter somehow puts it all back into perspective. How differently God sees our petty strivings.

Dear Friend

This summer a special occasion took place. It was just another prize-giving and yet so very strange. It was not the headmaster that made it unusual; he stood, and in time-honoured fashion read out the list of those who had achieved in outstanding ways. It was not the prizes that set this occasion apart – the usual display of books and certificates was in evidence, and it was not even the children, although it has to be said that this was not a typical school assembly.

No, it was the *achievements* that made this particular prize-giving so different. As the head read them out, none who were present had any doubt that the feats that these teenage children had performed were outstanding. But everybody knew there was hardly a child of any age, in any school in the country, that could not have done any one of them.

The audience listened as the head read the names and reasons why these particular pupils had won a prize. 'Mark because he has fed himself all this term, and Susan who has recited a poem and can brush her teeth.'

The school was one that cared for severely physically and mentally disadvantaged children. As some shuffled and others danced to collect their trophies there was hardly a dry eye in the place. And yet this was more than just emotion; it was somehow a spiritual event, somehow of another world. Why was it so different?

I believe the key to it was that this headmaster was doing something that is unusual today. He was recognising worth by standards which are alien to our society.

In our culture we are used to prize-givings. They are occasions when we acknowledge those who have out-performed the normal man and woman by achieving extraordinary feats. Not many of us will ever walk up the steps of a stage in Hollywood to collect our Oscar, or stand on a winner's rostrum clutching a gold medal as the world listens to our national anthem.

And you may therefore think it patronising to honour those who have learnt to brush their teeth. But I can only tell you on that day it seemed as if God himself was giving those commendations. As if far above our little world with its preoccupation with physical beauty, with power and prestige, there was another place where the ceremony, the standards – and the awards were different.

No one can make you feel inferior without your consent.

Eleanor Roosevelt

SUCCESS

Success is being friendly when another needs
    a friend ...
It's in the cheery words you speak and in the coins
    you lend ...
Success is not alone in skill and deeds of doing
    great ...
It's in the roses that you plant beside your garden
    gate ...
Success is in the way you walk the paths of life each
    day ...
It's in the little things you do and in the things you
    say ...
Success is in the glad hello you give your fellow
    man ...
It's in the laughter of your home and all the joys you
    plan ...
Success is not getting rich or rising high to fame ...
It's not alone in winning goals which all men hope to
    claim ...
It's in the person you are each day through happiness
    or care ...
It's in the happy words you speak and in the smile
    you wear ...
Success is being big of heart and clean and broad of
    mind ...
It's in being faithful to your friends and to the
    stranger, kind.

Anon.

CHAPTER TWELVE

They'll learn much more …

* * *

When, as a child, I laughed and wept, time crept.
When, as a youth, I dreamed and talked, time
    walked.
When I became a full-grown man, time ran.
And later, as I older grew, time flew.
Soon I shall find, while travelling on, time gone.
Will Christ have saved my soul by then?

Anon.

Youth is not a time of life, it is a state of mind, a product of imagination, a vigour of the emotion, a predominate of courage over timidity, an appetite for adventure.

Nobody grows old by living a number of years. People grow old when they desert their ideals. Years wrinkle the skin, but to give up enthusiasm wrinkles the soul. Worry, self-doubt, fear and anxiety, these are the culprits that bow the head and break the heart.

Whether sixteen or seventy, there exists in the heart of every person who loves life, the thrill of a new challenge, the insatiable appetite for what is coming next. You are as young as your faith, and as old as your doubts.

So long as your heart receives from your head messages that reflect beauty, courage, joy and excitement, you are young. When your thinking becomes clouded with pessimism and prevents you from taking risks, then you are old ... and may God have mercy on your soul.

Anon.

God says: I like youngsters. I want people to be like them. I don't like old people unless they are still children. I want only children in my kingdom: this has been decreed from the beginning of time.

Youngsters – twisted, humped, wrinkled, white-bearded – all kinds of youngsters, but youngsters ... I like them because they are still growing, they are still improving.

They are on the road, they are on their way.

But with grown-ups there is nothing to expect any more.

They will no longer grow ...

It is disastrous – grown-ups think they have arrived.

Michel Quoist

The Hebrews regarded life as complete when it was full of days and riches and honour. Age was looked upon as a sign of favour. Whenever a nation becomes unspiritual, it reverses this order, the demand is not for old age but for youth. This reversal in the modern life of today is indicative of apostasy, not of advance.

Oswald Chambers

For age is opportunity no less
than youth itself,
though in another dress.
And as the evening
twilight fades away
the sky is filled with
stars, invisible by day.

Henry Wadsworth Longfellow

How I have laughed over the years at Bill Cosby. His TV shows, albums and books have been so entertaining. Here is a short excerpt from his book Time Flies.

The reason we must be tolerant with older people who have lost some of their hearing or vision or mind is simply that *we* will almost certainly have such loss if we enjoy the good fortune to live long enough to fall apart. In fact, life plays a great joke on middle-aged people: it teaches them how foolish they were when they swore years ago that they would never become as crazy as their parents. A study of your mother and father is a worthwhile thing to do because it gives you a nice little preview of your own late-blooming looniness.

Avenge yourself – live long enough to be a problem to your kids.

Be kind to your children. They may choose your rest homes.

Notice seen in a café in Palm Springs

WARNING

When I am an old woman I shall wear purple
With a red hat which doesn't go, and doesn't suit me,
And I shall spend my pension on brandy and summer
    gloves
And satin sandals, and say we've no money for
    butter.
I shall sit down on the pavement when I'm tired
And gobble up samples in shops and press alarm bells
And run my stick along the public railings
And make up for the sobriety of my youth.
I shall go out in my slippers in the rain
And pick the flowers in other people's gardens
And learn to spit.

You can wear terrible shirts and grow more fat
And eat three pounds of sausages at a go
Or only bread and pickle for a week
And hoard pens and pencils and beer mats and things
    in boxes.

But now we must have clothes that keep us dry
And pay our rent and not swear in the street
And set a good example for the children.
We must have friends to dinner and read the papers.

But maybe I ought to practise a little now?
So people who know me are not too shocked and
    surprised
When I am old, and start to wear purple.

Jenny Joseph

Listen to your father who gave you life and don't despise your mother's experience when she is old. (!)

Proverbs 23:22

*M*ore from Bill Cosby ...

WASTED ON THE YOUNG

At least my wife and her cuddler are growing older together: we're in sync because neither of us has dived into one of the many fountains of youth that are bubbling all over this age-feared land. We haven't panicked about getting older and started trying to look like our children. Last year, Americans spent more than one billion dollars on lotions, potions, and surgery so that they could be confused with their children instead of just being confused by them.

A few days ago on television, I saw a commercial for a liquid detergent. Two different women were displaying their hands side by side for the nation to admire.

'Can you tell the mother's hands from her daughter's?' an announcer asked me.

'Of course,' I replied. 'The daughter's hands are the ones that have just been in her mother's wallet.'

What is the point of all this? That mothers should be impersonating their daughters? That all of us should be one big happy teenage generation? Can you imagine a more frightening horror film than one in which all the adults in America turned into teenagers? This is a wonderful country, but the people in it are quite insane about reversing the ageing process. They are trying to wake up every morning heading for yesterday. Where will it all end? Since there seems to be a stampede back to the womb, it will all end with one foetus trying to call out to another, 'I'm less developed than you!'

I know one woman who puts bee pollen on her skin to keep it looking young. She is now a woman who could fertilize a flower with a sneeze, but she is driven to turn back the clock to Teenage Saving Time. Other women are putting potato peelings and tea bags on their eyelids; some are covering their faces with Italian mud; and a newspaper recently told of a woman who put cement on her face as a cosmetic mask and couldn't remove it.

One of these days, I will walk into somebody's home and ask, 'What's that new statue in your living room, Newt?'

'That's no statue,' he will say, 'that's Mother. Lovely skin, don't you think?'

'Absolutely. Not a pothole in sight.'

For twenty years, I have known one particular woman, who now does not look anything like the woman I met twenty years ago or the woman I knew three months ago. She has had plastic surgery so often that her features have changed and she is now wearing someone else's face; the essence of her has disappeared. She is very happy because she doesn't look old. She does, however, look mismatched. She is a new kind of female impersonator.

Plastic surgery has been creating hundreds of thousands of people like this, people whose parts don't match, people who seem to have been assembled by astigmatic elves. If you put a boyish face on a man of seventy-three who can't bend over, you have a new kind of centaur – and the horse's ass is the man who had the surgery.

IT'S MUCH LATER THAN YOU THINK

Everything is so much further away than it used to be. It is twice as far to the corner, and they have added a hill, so I've noticed. I've given up running for the bus, as it leaves faster than it used to. It seems to me they are making stairs steeper than they used to in the old days. Have you noticed the smaller print they now use in the newspaper? There is no sense asking anyone to read aloud, everyone talks so low I can hardly hear them. And material in dresses is so skimpy now, especially around the waist and hips. It is almost impossible to reach my shoelaces. Even people are changing. They are so much younger than they used to be when I was their age. On the other hand, people my own age are so much older than I am. I ran into a classmate the other day, and she had aged so much she didn't even recognise me. I got to thinking about the poor thing while I was combing my hair this morning, and in doing so I glanced at my own reflection. Confound it, they don't make good mirrors like they used to!

Perspective is how we look at life, ourselves, and our problems. Some look at ageing as a unique opportunity for fun. Those who grow older but insist on blaming it on a changing world react with a perspective, too. They deny their own participation in something none of us can avoid – ageing – and refuse to take responsibility for their own human frailties. Most of us would give almost anything to be able to change reality, especially when our kids have sent us into a tailspin and we aren't sure we will survive (or even if we want to survive!). In such a situation, ageing and weight problems tend to seem insurmountable. Just keep in mind that you are not alone; there are thousands of others in just the same kind of circumstances you find yourself. God will take care of you, just as He cares for others. We're all somewhere in that in-between age, fighting the battles of weight and senility. Remember, the Lord is right beside us, encouraging, admonishing, and setting goals for us. Give your best to God, and then forget about your pounds and years. No one is too heavy or too old to need and receive God's love.

Barbara Johnson

Warned from the body to depart,
What shall I of my God desire?
Pardon and grace to keep my heart
Till thou my ready soul require.

All that is past, my God, forgive;
For the short time to come defend;
And strengthening without sin to live,
Oh bless me with a peaceful end.

Meet for the fellowship above,
The glories of eternity,
Thy servant, Lord, with ease remove,
And let me fall asleep in thee.

Do thou, if so thy love ordain,
Gently the knot of life untie;
And free from sin, and free from pain,
In mercy's arms I sweetly die.

Charles Wesley

THE GREAT LOVER

These I have loved:
      White plates and cups, clean gleaming,
Ringed with blue lines; and feathery, faery dust;
Wet roofs, beneath the lamp-light; the strong crust
Of friendly bread; and many-tasting food;
Rainbows; and the blue bitter smoke of wood;
And radiant raindrops couching in cool flowers;
And flowers themselves, that sway through sunny
    hours,
Dreaming of moths that drink them under the
    moon;
Then, the cool kindliness of sheets, that soon
Smooth away trouble; and the rough male kiss
Of blankets; grainy wood; live hair that is
Shining and free; blue-massing clouds; the keen
Unpassioned beauty of a great machine;
The benison of hot water; furs to touch;
The smell of old clothes; and other such –
The comfortable smell of friendly fingers,
Hair's fragrance, and the musty reek that lingers
About dead leaves and last year's ferns ...
And washen stones, gay for an hour; the cold
Graveness of iron; moist black earthen mould;
Sleep; and high places; footprints in the dew;
And oaks; and brown horse-chestnuts, glossy-new;
And new-peeled sticks; and shining pools on grass; –
All these have been my loves. And these shall pass,
Whatever passes not, in the great hour,
Nor all my passion, all my prayers, have power
To hold them with me through the gate of Death.

They'll play deserter, turn with the traitor breath,
Break the high bond we made, and sell Love's trust
And sacramented covenant to the dust.

– Oh, never a doubt but, somewhere, I shall wake,
And give what's left of love again, and make
New friends, now strangers …
                    But the best I've known
Stays here, and changes, breaks, grows old, is blown
About the winds of the world, and fades from brains
Of living men, and dies.
                    Nothing remains.

O dear my loves, O faithless, once again
This one last fight I give; that after men
Shall know, and later lovers, far-removed,
Praise you, 'all these were lovely': say, 'He loved'.

Rupert Brooke

Sir Harry Secombe was Roy's best man at our wedding, and has always been a wonderful, faithful friend to our family. I was delighted that he allowed me to include the following poem, which he was commissioned to write for a Songs of Praise *programme*.

HARRY'S POEM

I want the mornings to last longer
and the twilight to linger

I want to clutch the present to my bosom
and never let it go

I resent the tyranny of the clock in the hall
nagging me to get on with the day

I am a time traveller
but a traveller who would rather walk than fly

And yet;
there is a lot to be said for growing old

The major battles in life are over
though minor skirmishes may still occur

There is an armistice of the heart
a truce with passion

Compromise becomes preferable to conflict
and old animosities blur with time

There is still one last hurdle to cross
and the joy of your life measures your reluctance to
   approach it

But if you have lived your life with love
there will be nothing to fear

Because a warm welcome will await you on the other
   side.

When a man dies he clutches in his hands only
that which he has given away in his lifetime.

A PSALM OF LIFE

What the Heart of the Young Man
said to the Psalmist

Tell me not, in mournful numbers,
'Life is but an empty dream!'
For the soul is dead that slumbers,
And things are not what they seem.

Life is real! Life is earnest!
And the grave is not its goal;
'Dust thou art, to dust returnest'
Was not spoken of the soul.

Not enjoyment, and not sorrow,
Is our destined end or way;
But to act, that each to-morrow
Find us farther than to-day.

Art is long, and Time is fleeting,
And our hearts, though stout and brave,
Still, like muffled drums, are beating
Funeral marches to the grave.

In the world's broad field of battle,
In the bivouac of Life,
Be not like dumb, driven cattle!
Be a hero in the strife!

Trust no Future, howe'er pleasant!
Let the dead Past bury its dead!
Act – act in the living Present!
Heart within, and God o'erhead!

Lives of great men all remind us
We can make our lives sublime,
And, departing, leave behind us
Footprints on the sands of time; –

Footprints, that perhaps another,
Sailing o'er life's solemn main,
A forlorn and shipwrecked brother,
Seeing, shall take heart again.

Let us, then, be up and doing,
With a heart for any fate;
Still achieving, still pursuing,
Learn to labour and to wait.

Henry Wadsworth Longfellow

I want to die living – not live dying.

CHAPTER THIRTEEN

What a wonderful world?

✽ ✽ ✽

The question mark is mine. I refer back to Louis Armstrong's comments, which I quoted at the beginning. 'It seems to me it ain't the world that's so bad, but what we're doing to it and all I'm saying is, see what a wonderful world it would be if only we'd give it a chance ...'

Here are the words of a song that impressed me when Sir Cliff Richard made it famous some years ago. I imagined I was looking down on the world from an aeroplane, where everything looked neat and clean and far removed from the pain and problems of life.

From a distance
The world looks blue and green
And the snow-capped mountains so white.
From a distance
The ocean meets the stream
And the eagle takes to flight.
From a distance there is harmony
And it echoes through the land,

It's the voice of hope
It's the voice of peace
It's the voice of everyone.

From a distance we all have enough
And no one is in need.
There are no guns
No bombs and no disease
No hungry mouths to feed.
For a moment we must be instruments
Marching in a common band.

Playing songs of hope
Playing songs of peace
They're the songs of everyone.

God is watching us from a distance.

From a distance you look like my friend
Even though we are at war.
From a distance I can't quite comprehend
What all this war is for.
What we need is love and harmony
Let it echo through the lands.

It's the hope of hopes
It's the love of loves –
It's the heart of everyone.

Julie A. Gold

O Lord, the clouds are gathering,
the fire of judgement burns.
How we have fallen.
O Lord, you stand appalled to see
your laws of love so scorned
and lives so broken.

> Have mercy Lord
> Forgive us Lord
> Restore us Lord
> Revive your church again
> Let justice flow
> Like a river
> And righteousness
> Like a never-failing stream.

O Lord, over the nations now,
where is the dove of peace?
Her wings are broken.
O Lord, while precious children starve,
the tools of war increase;
their bread is stolen.

O Lord, dark pow'rs are poised to flood
our streets with hate and fear;
we must awaken!
O Lord, let love reclaim the lives
that sin would sweep away,
and let your kingdom come.

Yet, O Lord, your glorious cross shall tower
triumphant in this land,
evil confounding.
Through the fire your suffering church displays
the glories of her Christ:
praises resounding.

> Have mercy Lord
> Forgive us Lord
> Restore us Lord
> Revive your church again
> Let justice flow
> Like a river
> And righteousness
> Like a never-failing stream.

Graham Kendrick

As long as we fail to do anything positive to
alleviate the suffering of others we are merely
continuing to contribute to it.

Steve Chalke

LORD OF ALL

Lord of the complex web of life,
Creator of a kingdom where all things
are next of kin to all other things,
you placed us carefully within your system,
and called us to represent you there.
Create in us clean hearts, O God,
and put new and right spirits within us.

We confess that we have followed our father Adam,
and forged our lives
according to plans of our own.
We have become a law to ourselves,
with little reference to you,
our brothers and sisters,
or your creation – our next of kin.
Create in us clean hearts, O God,
and put new and right spirits within us.

We have abused your gift of this earth,
the work of your own fingers,
the place where you rest your feet,
the home where your Son walked,
the fragile mother of us all.
Create in us clean hearts, O God,
and put new and right spirits within us.

For the arrogance
which blithely sweeps your creation aside
for the ignorance
which tampers with the very web of life,
for the greed
which exhausts and destroys our resources,
for the injustices
which deny essentials to the poor,
for the selfishness
which will not share your plenty,
for the insolence
by which we take for ourselves
the right to threaten all life
in nuclear war:
For these and all our crimes
Against you and your creation,
Lord Jesus Christ, forgive us.

For the compassion, to tread gently,
trust, to share generously,
courage, to act justly,
and faith, to live simply:
We ask you,
encouraged by the gift of yourself
for us and all creation,
and the plan of your Father
to bring all things together again
with you as Head. Amen.

Aub Podlich

None can be at peace while others wallow in poverty and insecurity.

Nelson Mandela

Myth: With food-producing resources in so much of the world stretched to the limit, there's simply not enough food to go around. Unfortunately some people will just have to go hungry.

Our Response: The world today produces enough grain alone to provide every human being on the planet with thirty-five hundred calories a day. That's enough to make most people fat! And this estimate does not even count many other commonly eaten foods – vegetables, beans, nuts, root crops, fruits, grass-fed meats, and fish. In fact, if all foods are considered together, enough is available to provide at least 4.3 pounds of food per person a day. That includes two and a half pounds of grain, beans, and nuts; about a pound of fruits and vegetables; and nearly another pound of meat, milk and eggs.

Abundance, not scarcity, best describes the supply of food in the world today. Increases in food production during the past thirty-five years have outstripped the world's unprecedented population growth by about 16 per cent. Indeed, mountains of unsold grain on world markets have pushed prices strongly downward over the past three and a half decades. Grain prices rose briefly during the early 1990s, as bad weather coincided with policies geared toward reducing over-production, but remained well below the highs observed in the early sixties and mid-seventies.

Frances Moore Lappé, Joseph Collins and Peter Rosset

It is always the oppressor, not the oppressed who dictates the form of the struggle.

Nelson Mandela

DESTROYERS ARE PEOPLE TOO

If everyone got what he deserved, who could ever escape whipping?
Shakespeare in *Hamlet*

What do we call a man who comes with great power to take our land, tears the heart out of it for his own selfish greed, and then gives it back to us without its heart? Such a man you are to call your enemy, say the Lord. And what are we to do with such a person? The Lord replies: 'You are to love him; he is your enemy!' 'But, Lord, he is my enemy,' we protest. 'Yes', says Jesus, 'and *you* were mine!'

'A tree has no value unless it can be turned into profit', a man said. His company proposed to feed a pulp mill 1.8 million tonnes of Tasmania's forests each year, and spew the pollutants into the sea. I don't even know the man, but already I don't like him. But, God, I can't stay your friend if I don't love him!

What does it mean to love someone you don't like, and about whom you have already made severe moral judgments?

It means, first, to dismount from your high horse! There are few people who are more self-righteous than born-again Greenies – of whom I am one! Human beings bear collective guilt toward the environmental problems that earth faces. As a species, we have become to earth what AIDS has become to us all! We are *all* guilty! God apportions blame – not lesser or greater degrees of it.

A nun from a large Catholic hospital in Brisbane was asked whether she as a religious person felt any moral outrage against people with AIDS. She replied: 'I am only conscious of this, that I in my life have done many things which were wrong, and I fully deserve God's punishment. As one who has been shown God's grace, I can only try to bring a similar grace to those who are in need, no matter what the circumstances.' Love begins with such humility before God.

To love someone means to actively promote their ultimate good, whether we like them or not. Some enemies we may never come to like; but Christ makes it quite clear that, if we cannot learn to love such enemies, then we disqualify ourselves from marching in the troops he leads in this war.

Christ commands love. Such a command may seem almost ludicrous to us who have been raised on a notion of 'falling in love', as if love is a case of being seized by something beyond our control. But Christian love is not a feeling or emotion, as liking is. Christian love is birthed in a will which has fallen captive to Christ, and now expresses the nature of Christ. Christian love can be learnt. Paul once wrote to Titus to 'teach the older women to ... train the younger women to love their husbands and children' (Titus 2:3, 4).

Despite what we *feel* about people, despite our disagreement with their sins, we cannot ever neglect to seek ways of actively promoting their highest good. No one can spell that out exactly in practical terms for us. Each situation and opportunity will be different. And, because I know that I don't really want to love certain people, I need to begin with prayer that God will draw me closer to himself, that I might the more faithfully imitate him.

Aub Podlich

When people stop believing in God they don't then believe in nothing – they believe in anything and everything.

G. K. Chesterton

We have such a responsibility to our children to show them The Way. I think the words in the following song are the most powerful Graham Kendrick has ever written. I often quote the lines: 'We have sacrificed the children / On the altar of our gods'. Awesome words!

> Who can sound the depth of sorrow
> In the Father heart of God
> For the children we've rejected
> For the lives so deeply scarred?
> And each light that we've extinguished
> Has brought darkness to our land
> Upon our nation, upon our nation
> Have mercy Lord.
>
> We have scorned the truth you gave us,
> We have bowed to other lords.
> We have sacrificed the children
> On the altar of our gods.
> O let truth again shine on us,
> Let your holy fear descend:
> Upon our nation, upon our nation
> Have mercy, Lord.

(men)
Who can stand before your anger?
Who can face your piercing eyes?
For you love the weak and helpless,
And you hear the victims' cries.
(all)
Yes, you are a God of justice,
And your judgment surely comes:
Upon our nation, upon our nation
Have mercy, Lord.

(women)
Who will stand against the violence?
Who will comfort those who mourn?
In an age of cruel rejection,
Who will build for love a home?
(all)
Come and shake us into action,
Come and melt our hearts of stone;
Upon your people, upon your people
Have mercy, Lord.

Who can sound the depth of mercy
In the Father heart of God?
For there is a Man of sorrows
Who for sinners shed his blood.
He can heal the wounds of nations,
He can wash the guilty clean:
Because of Jesus, because of Jesus
Have mercy, Lord.

At the end of the twentieth century most of
us will not have to repent of the great evils
we have done but of the apathy that
prevented us from doing anything at all.

Martin Luther King

She calls out to the man on the street
'Sir, can you help me?
It's cold and I've nowhere to sleep
Is there somewhere you can tell me?'

He walks on, doesn't look back
He pretends he can't hear her
Starts to whistle as he crosses the street
Seems embarrassed to be there.

Oh, think twice, it's another day for you and me in
    paradise
Oh, think twice, it's another day for you and me in
    paradise.

She calls out to the man on the street
He can see she's been crying
She's got blisters on the soles of her feet
Can't walk, but she's trying.

Oh, think twice …

You can tell from the lines on her face
You can see that she's been there
Probably been moved on from every place
'Cos she didn't fit in there.

Oh, think twice …

Phil Collins

We all long for heaven where God is, but we
have it in our power to be happy with Him
at this very moment. Being happy with Him
now means loving as He does, helping like
He helps, giving as He gives, serving as He
serves, rescuing as He rescues, being with
Him twenty-four hours a day – touching
Him in His distressing disguise.

Mother Teresa of Calcutta

However, encountering our passionate God faces us with an even bigger challenge. He calls the church to live out his passion in the world around, modelling his love and justice not just in our relationships together as Christians but also through our commitment to those in need. He calls us to share his priorities in embracing a hurting world, treating the most unlovely of people with dignity and affirmation. He challenges us to step outside the comfortable safety of what is familiar to us. He calls us to risk sharing in his zeal for love and justice to be worked out in society, investing into building a sense of community amongst people who are very alone.

When faced with all of this, it is understandable that we might be tempted to retreat into just pursuing our personal lives. Maybe it is all a bit daunting, or our individual sphere of influence seems too limited. However, it is worth remembering that one snowflake on its own melts on the cheek but a snowstorm can stop the traffic! In other words, together with each other and God we can make a difference. The challenge and the wonder of encountering a God with passion is that we can never truly be the same again.

Fran Beckett

Time is cluttered with the wreckage of communities which surrendered to hatred and violence. For the salvation of our nation and the salvation of mankind, we must follow another way ... To our most bitter opponents we say: 'We shall match your capacity to inflict suffering by our capacity to endure suffering. We shall meet your physical force with soul force. Do to us what you will, and we shall continue to love you ... Throw us in jail, and we shall still love you. Send your hooded perpetrators of violence into our community at the midnight hour and beat us and leave us half dead, and we shall still love you. But be ye assured that we will wear you down by our capacity to suffer ...' Love is the most durable power in the world.

Martin Luther King

INDIFFERENCE

When Jesus came to Golgotha they hanged Him on a
    tree,
They drove great nails through hands and feet, and
    made a Calvary;
They crowned Him with a crown of thorns, red were
    His wounds and deep,
For those were crude and cruel days, and human
    flesh was cheap.

When Jesus came to Birmingham they simply passed
    Him by,
They never hurt a hair of Him, they only let Him die;
For men had grown more tender, and they would
    not give Him pain,
They only just passed down the street, and left Him
    in the rain.

Still Jesus cried, 'Forgive them, for they know not
    what they do,'
And still it rained the wintry rain that drenched Him
    through and through.
The crowds went home and left the streets without a
    soul to see,
And Jesus crouched against a wall and cried for
    Calvary.

G. A. Studdert Kennedy

Come and see, come and see
Come and see the King of love;
See the purple robe and crown of thorns he wears
Soldiers mock, rulers sneer
As He lifts the cruel cross;
Lone and friendless now he climbs towards the hill.

We worship at your feet
Where wrath and mercy meet
And a guilty world is washed by love's pure stream
For us He was made sin,
Oh, help me take it in.
Deep wounds of love cry out 'Father forgive'.
I worship, I worship
The Lamb who was slain.

Come and weep, come and mourn
for your sin that pierced him there
so much deeper than the wounds of thorn and nail
All our pride, all our greed,
All our fallenness and shame
And the Lord has laid the punishment on Him.

We worship at your feet
Where wrath and mercy meet
And a guilty world is washed by love's pure stream
For us He was made sin,
Oh, help me take it in.
Deep wounds of love cry out 'Father forgive'.
I worship, I worship
The Lamb who was slain.

Man of Heaven, born to earth
Restore us to your heaven
Here we bow in awe beneath your searching eyes.
From your tears comes our joy,
From your death our life shall spring;
By your resurrection power we shall rise.

We worship at your feet
Where wrath and mercy meet
And a guilty world is washed by love's pure stream
For us He was made sin,
Oh, help me take it in.
Deep wounds of love cry out 'Father forgive'.
I worship, I worship
The Lamb who was slain.

Graham Kendrick

Then Jesus said, 'Come to me, all of you
who are weary and carry heavy burdens, and
I will give you rest. Take my yoke upon you.
Let me teach you, because I am humble and
gentle, and you will find rest for your souls.
For my yoke fits perfectly and the burden I
give you is light.'

Matthew 11:28–30

Peter Greave wrote a memoir of his life with leprosy, a disease he contracted while stationed in India. He returned to England, half-blind and partially paralysed, to live on a compound run by Anglican sisters. Unable to work, an outcast from society, he turned bitter. He thought of suicide. He made elaborate plans to escape the compound, but always backed out because he had nowhere to go. One morning, uncharacteristically, he got up very early and strolled the grounds. Hearing a buzzing noise, he followed it to the chapel, where sisters were praying for the patients whose names were written on its walls. Among the names, he found his own. Somehow that experience of connection, of linking, changed his life. He felt wanted. He felt graced.

Religious faith – for all its problems, despite its maddening tendency to replicate ungrace – lives on because we sense the numinous beauty of a gift undeserved that comes at unexpected moments from Outside. Refusing to believe that our lives of guilt and shame lead to nothing but annihilation, we hope against hope for another place run by different rules. We grow up hungry for love, and in ways so deep as to remain unexpressed we long for our Maker to love us.

Philip Yancey

He who cannot forgive another breaks the bridge over which he must pass himself.

George Herbert

So don't get tired of doing what is good. Don't get discouraged and give up, for we will reap a harvest of blessing at the appropriate time. Whenever we have the opportunity we should do good to everyone, especially to our Christian brothers and sisters.

Paul, writing to the Galatian Christians (Galatians 6:9–10)

While women weep as they do now, I'll fight;

while little children go hungry as they do now, I'll fight;

while men go to prison, in and out, in and out, I'll fight;

while there yet remains one dark soul without the light of God,

I'll fight – I'll fight to the very end!

General William Booth, in his 82nd year at a public meeting on 9 May 1912 at the Albert Hall, London – his last speech

If we are to better the future we must disturb the present.

Catherine Booth

His presence is not bound
To vast cathedrals and the light that falls
Through many-tinted glass. His voice and touch are
    found
Within the poorest doors, the humblest walls.

He sits at table with the tired and poor,
He shares the fireplace with the spent and old,
He keeps with suffering a vigil sure,
And plays with childhood in the summer's gold.

His feet refuse no threshold, want and care
Do not repulse him, no, nor even sin.
Wherever need is waiting, he is there,
Where love invites, he enters in.

Anon.

Such a lovely world was made for you and me
Wondrous life to taste touch smell hear and see
But one glance from outside looking at our world
    state
Clearly displays we don't appreciate it at all.

Rain your love down won't you rain down your love
Let it drench us like the sun from above

Such ability inside you and me
Made to do anything and be all we can be
But one bird's eye view at us does show, oh it shows
That against God's plan we've let it go. Oh no!

Rain your love down won't you rain down your love
Let it drench us like the sun from above
Rain your love down let it rain down today
So that it may wash all our sins away.

You'd think the signs would make a difference
Oh, make a difference
You'd think fire next time instead of rain
Would cause us to make a change
The world has gone insane.

Rain your love down won't you rain down your love
Let it drench us like the sun from above
Rain your love down let it rain down today
So that it may wash all our sins away.
Let it rain
Rain your love down oh will you let it start
wash the wicked minds and the … I
know they're sick we know they're sick at heart yeah
rain down your love won't you let it rain
Rid this world of drugs disease crime and pain.

Clear our spirits give our minds new software
With your lessons on honour respect trust and care
Rain your love down I beg for human sake
for only you can get us out of this state.

Rain your love down on all mankind
Cos we are out of order and so out of line.

Stevie Wonder

NO PURE JOY:

Celebration in the Midst of Pain
– John 16:20

No matter how much we desire perfection and completeness, we need to embrace the fact of our limitations. In our broken world, things are less than what we would like them to be. And our own imperfections are writ large on all that we do. This need not drive us to despair. Nor should it prevent us from purposeful activity. We can still do what we must even when a totally satisfactory conclusion eludes us.

Nouwen reminds us that 'there is no such thing as clear-cut pure joy.' Our experience of love, no matter how loyal or ecstatic, is marked by selfishness and pain. Even our spiritual experiences do not yield the fruit of perfection. These experiences are frequently marred by doubt and guilt.

Such is our lot. We reach for the sky, but cannot inherit the earth. We long for the good, but frequently produce something that is a pale version of our best intentions. We are like a beautiful princess with feet of clay or like a powerful prince with a physical impediment. Made for God's highest intention, we sometimes fritter away our calling and opportunities. Made for greatness, we easily become side-tracked by our success and power. A profound sadness thus underlies our life.

But our sadness can be turned into joy. This is not a joy that comes from a perpetual striving, but a joy that comes in the midst of our pain. It's the joy of being loved in spite of our imperfections. It's the joy that comes from forgiveness. It's the joy that comes as a gift that we don't deserve. It's the joy that comes as a surprise in spite of ourselves.

Thus in the midst of our pain we can celebrate. In the midst of our broken world we can still dance.

Charles Ringma

Lord, make me a channel of your peace
Where there is hatred, let me sow love,
Where there is injury, pardon
Where there is doubt, faith
Where there is despair, hope
Where there is darkness, light
Where there is sadness, joy.

O Divine Master, grant that I may not so much seek
    to be consoled as to console
not so much to be understood as to understand
not so much to be loved as to love;
for it is in giving that we receive,
it is in pardoning that we are pardoned,
it is in dying that we awake to eternal life.

St Francis of Assisi

CHAPTER FOURTEEN

A wonderful world, oh yeah!

✳ ✳ ✳

For the LORD your God is bringing you into a good land of flowing streams and pools of water, with springs that gush forth in the valleys and the hills. It is a land of wheat and barley, of grape vines, fig trees, pomegranates, olives and honey. It is a land where food is plentiful and nothing is lacking. It is a land where iron is as common as stone, and copper is abundant in the hills. When you have eaten your fill, praise the LORD your God for the good land he has given you.

Deuteronomy 8:7–10

Once there was a man who dared God to speak.

Burn the bush like You did for Moses, God ... and I will follow,

Collapse the wall like You did for Joshua, God ... and I will fight.

Still the waves like You did on Galilee, God ... and I will listen.

And so the man sat by a bush, near a wall, close to the sea, and waited for God to speak.

And God heard the man, so God answered.

He sent fire, not for a bush, but for a church.

He brought down a wall, not of brick, but of sin.

He stilled a storm, not of the sea, but of a soul. And God waited for the man to respond.

And He waited ... and He waited ... and waited.

But because the man was looking at bushes, not hearts; bricks and not lives, seas and not souls, he decided that God had done nothing.

Finally he looked to God and asked, 'Have You lost your power?'

And God looked at him and said, 'Have you lost your hearing?'

Max Lucado

*I*found this prayer when I was a teenager and kept
a copy of it in my purse for years until it fell to
pieces. Great to read, but not so easy to practise!

> Christ has no hands but our hands
> To do His work today;
> Christ has no feet but our feet
> To lead men in His way;
> Christ has no tongue but our tongue
> To tell men how He died;
> Christ has no help but our help
> To bring them to His side.

Anon.

*T*he following hymn was a favourite of Roy's. It
was one he sang in church as a young boy and
although it might sound rather sentimental now,
the message is clear. He asked for it to be sung on a
TV programme with Alan Titchmarsh shortly before
he died.

> Have you had a kindness shown?
> Pass it on!
> 'Twas not given for you alone;
> Pass it on!
> Let it travel down the years,
> Let it wipe another's tears,
> Till in heaven the deed appears;
> Pass it on!

Did you hear the loving word?
Pass it on!
Like the singing of a bird?
Pass it on!
Let its music live and grow,
Let it cheer another's woe,
You have reaped what others sow –
Pass it on!

Be not selfish in your greed,
Pass it on!
Look upon your brother's need,
Pass it on!
Live for self you live in vain;
Live for Christ you live again;
Live with him, with him you reign –
Pass it on!

Anon.

Great is thy faithfulness, O God my Father,
There is no shadow of turning with Thee;
Thou changest not, Thy compassions, they fail not;
As thou hast been thou forever wilt be.

Great is thy faithfulness!
Great is thy faithfulness!
Morning by morning new mercies I see;
All I have needed thy hand hath provided,
Great is thy faithfulness, Lord, unto me!

Summer and winter, and springtime and harvest,
Sun, moon and stars in their courses above,
Join with all nature in manifold witness
To thy great faithfulness, mercy and love.

Pardon for sin and a peace that endureth,
Thine own dear presence to cheer and to guide;
Strength for today and bright hope for tomorrow,
Blessings all mine, with ten thousand beside!

Thomas Obadiah Chisholm

'SHEPHERD BOY'S SONG'

He that is down needs fear no fall,
He that is low no pride,
He that is humble shall ever
Have God to be his guide.
I am content with what I have
Little be it, or much
And Lord, contentment still I crave
Because thou savest such.
Fullness to such, a burden us,
That go on pilgrimage;
Have little, and hereafter bliss,
Is best from age to age.

John Bunyan

I have learned how to get along happily whether I have much or little. I know how to live on almost nothing or with everything. I have learned the secret of living in every situation with a full stomach or empty, with plenty or little. For I can do everything with the help of Christ who gives me the strength I need.

Philippians 4:11–13

Oh, I got plenty of nothin'
And nothin's plenty for me.
I got no car, got no mule
I got no misery.
The folks with plenty o' plenty,
Got a lock on the door
'Fraid somebody's a-goin' to rob 'em
While dey's out a makin' more
What for?

I got no lock on the door
(That's no way to be)
They can steal the rug from the floor
That's OK with me
'Cause the things I prize
Like the stars in the skies are all free.

Oh, I got plenty of nothin'
And nothin's plenty for me.
I got my gal, got my song
Got heaven the whole day long
(No use complainin')
Got my gal, got my Lord,
Got my song.

George Gershwin

Be kind and merciful. Let no one ever come to you without coming away better and happier. Be the living expression of God's kindness: kindness in your face, kindness in your eyes, kindness in your smile, kindness in your warm greeting. In the slums we are the light of God's kindness to the poor. To children, to the poor, to all who suffer and are lonely, give always a happy smile. Give them not only your care, but also your heart.

Mother Teresa of Calcutta

I bring every thought captive to the obedience of Christ.

2 Corinthians 10:5

In the USA, Christians have pendants and key rings and brooches with the letters WWJD, which stands for Who Would Jesus Do? If we really can bring every thought captive and ask that question, it would save us making a lot of mistakes!

Preach the gospel with all of your life and if necessary, with words.

St Francis of Assisi

O God, save us from offering unto Thee any prayer which we are not prepared that Thou shouldest answer. Save us from praying to see Thy face unless we are prepared that the vision should burn all the self out of us and make us let go our hateful little sins. Save us from asking for world vision, till we are ready to face world responsibilities. Save us from asking that we may follow Christ, without counting His lonely way, His utter sacrifice, His broken heart.

Take us very quietly each one and shut us in with thyself. It may be Thou art going to ask one of us to step right out to world adventure. It may be thou art going to ask a harder thing; that we should see all the need of the world and long to serve it in far-off lands, and yet stay just where we are. Only show us Thy will, and make us want to do it more than anything else in the world, and in that doing, find life. We ask it for the honour of Jesus Christ our Lord. Amen.

Leslie D. Weatherhead

MY SCHOOL PRAYER

Teach us, good Lord, to serve Thee as Thou deservest; to give and not to count the cost; to fight and not to heed the wounds; to toil and not to seek for rest; to labour and not to ask for any reward, save that of knowing that we do Thy will; through Jesus Christ our Lord. Amen.

Ignatius Loyola

May the mind of Christ my saviour
Live in me from day to day,
By his love and power controlling
All I do and say.

May the word of God dwell richly
In my heart from hour to hour,
So that all may see I triumph
Only through his power.

May the peace of God my father
Rule my life in everything,
That I may be calm to comfort
Sick and sorrowing.

May the love of Jesus fill me,
As the waters fill the sea;
Him exalting, self abasing
This is victory.

May I run the race before me,
Strong and brave to face the foe,
Looking only unto Jesus,
As I onward go.

Katie Barclay Wilkinson

A GAELIC BLESSING

Deep peace of the running wave to you,
Deep peace of the flowing air to you,
Deep peace of the quiet earth to you,
Deep peace of the shining stars to you,
Deep peace of the gentle night to you,
Moon and stars pour their healing light on you,
Deep peace of Christ the light of the world to you,
Deep peace of Christ to you.

Have a mustard seed faith,
Walk on water, sing a new song, spread joy,
Follow a rainbow.
Celebrate the dawn.
Rejoice in the Lord.
Welcome solitude.

Laugh heartily,
Feel enough to cry.
Reach out,
Share good news.
Start a conversation.
Plant a seed.
Mend a relationship.

Affirm others.
Forgive.
Seek forgiveness.

Let Jesus surprise you.
Bear someone's burden.
Love the unlovely.

Soar like an eagle.
Run the good race.
Walk without fainting.
Attempt the impossible.
Pray without ceasing.
Wait.
Never give up on God.

Anon.

I have chosen 'My Tribute' to finish the book. I wish I had written 'My Tribute' because it expresses so beautifully my declaration of faith, and my gratitude to God for all He has done in my life. In my younger years I had opportunities to sing it in public and if I could be singing it as I drew my last breath there would be a big smile on my face.

It is, therefore, my final offering, to give God the glory for His Wonderful World.

MY TRIBUTE

How can I say thanks
For all the things that you've done for me,
Things so undeserved and yet you gave
To prove your love for me.
The voices of a million angels
Could not express my gratitude –
All that I am, or ever hope to be
I owe it all to thee.

To God be the glory
To God be the glory
To God be the glory
For the things He has done
With His blood He has saved me
With His power He has raised me
To God be the Glory for the things He has done.

Just let me live my life,
Let it be pleasing Lord to Thee
Should I gain any praise
Let it go to Calvary.

With His blood He has saved me,
With His power He has raised me
To God be the glory for the things He has done.

Andrae Crouch

Index of first lines, titles and authors

✳ ✳ ✳